Plot
Twist

A personal
guide to surviving
life's unexpected
curveballs

Plot Twist

JANA FIRESTONE

Therapist and host of The Curious Life Podcast

ALLEN&UNWIN
SYDNEY·MELBOURNE·AUCKLAND·LONDON

First published in 2024

Allen & Unwin
Cammeraygal Country
83 Alexander Street
Crows Nest NSW 2065
Australia
Phone: (61 2) 8425 0100
Email: info@allenandunwin.com
Web: www.allenandunwin.com

Allen & Unwin acknowledges the Traditional Owners of the Country on which we live and work. We pay our respects to all Aboriginal and Torres Strait Islander Elders, past and present.

 A catalogue record for this book is available from the National Library of Australia

ISBN 978 1 76147 044 8

Set in 12/20 pt Minion Pro by Midland Typesetters, Australia
Printed and bound in Australia by the Opus Group

10 9 8 7 6 5 4 3 2 1

The paper in this book is FSC® certified. FSC® promotes environmentally responsible, socially beneficial and economically viable management of the world's forests.

This book is dedicated to my mother, Sybil (Raleigh) Firestone. For the magic of before and the sorrow of after—each pivotal chapters of my life. Though they were the very best and worst of my life's many plot twists, I am grateful for what I have learned through both.

Introduction

We can never be fully prepared for what life holds, but sometimes the universe completely pulls the rug from beneath our feet. I know firsthand what it feels like to have your entire existence thrown into chaos and confusion; to feel as if you have been plunged into the deepest depths of the ocean, forced under and holding your breath.

In the briefest of moments the ocean might release you from its grip just long enough for you to gulp in a lungful of air, before you're submerged again and thrashed against the rocks. It feels as if you're being flung around like a limp ragdoll, powerless against the surge.

That powerlessness is overwhelming. It's a state you can either submit to or fight against—but no matter which way you go, the outcome doesn't change. The plot has already twisted. You can't go back to the time before, no matter how hard you try.

When your life is suddenly, irrevocably disrupted—against your will, without warning—the experience can be so shocking that it takes a while to sink in. There can be numbness and pain, oceans of tears. There is often a giant question looming in the forefront of your mind as you plead to know, 'Why?'

We almost never see the plot twist coming. I certainly didn't get even a whiff of warning before my life changed.

It happened eight days after I turned 21.

I was living with my boyfriend Roscoe at the time, having just given up our tiny two-bedroom apartment in the heart of Toorak Village, right on the doorstep of all the nightlife we lived for, to move in with his mum on the other side of the West Gate Bridge for a while. We were just a few months into the transition, getting our bearings in the new neighbourhood and adjusting to living with three people in the house. I was working part-time on reception for a recruitment agency and as a bartender in a busy inner-city bar in South Melbourne. That bar was the central hub for all of our socialising. My boyfriend worked there, too, as well as a group of good friends, and we lived for the nights. I felt like I'd been launched into a sparkling adult life, throwing out the rules and boundaries of my recent adolescence, and revelling in my newfound freedom. I was living the typical hospitality life-style, working late and playing even later. After yet another busy weekend working in the bar, followed by a post-work all-nighter with the crew, my boyfriend and I were having a lazy Monday night in bed, watching TV.

It was almost 10 pm and I was hungover and tired. We were watching *Sex and the City*, my favourite show at the time. Watching it was a comfort to me. In that night's episode, one of the main characters, Miranda, experienced the sudden loss of her mother. It was a shock to her. As viewers we went on the journey with her through denial and avoidance, watching her deep emotions stir under the surface.

I remember being struck by the desire to ring my own mum in that moment, just to hear her voice and share how I was feeling. But it was late, and I decided not to. Something tugged at my brain, like a brief forewarning, hinting that I would regret not making that call. Instead, I pushed the feeling aside and went to sleep.

The next morning at around 7 am, I stepped out of the shower and returned to our bedroom. My boyfriend told me I had just missed a call from my dad. A throb of panic stabbed me in the stomach. I was hit with an instant knowledge that something was wrong.

Sitting on the bed in my towel, I called Dad back and listened as he calmly told me that Mum had been taken to hospital overnight. There was no panic in his voice, just a steady evenness, sounding just like Dad always did, as he told me, 'Mum lost consciousness overnight. I called the ambulance and they were able to revive her, but she's in emergency now at The Alfred Hospital.' An automatic howl bubbled up in the shape of the words, 'No, no, no, no!' I desperately wanted to rip his words right out of the air and force them into rewind, frantic to make it untrue.

My father, who is a doctor and very pragmatic and direct, told me the facts. Late in the evening, after finishing wrapping my brother's birthday present, Mum had been struggling to breathe. She quickly lost consciousness. Dad called an ambulance and began CPR. By the time the ambulance arrived she was unresponsive. The paramedics took over, trying to revive Mum. They were able to get her heart beating again, but it was unclear how long she had been without oxygen to her brain.

I scrambled to make sense of what I was hearing, while desperately resisting and rejecting the news at the same time.

It was my brother's eighteenth birthday that day. I had planned to go to work at my receptionist job, pick up his present—a very specific rugby ball that he'd had his eye on—and catch up with the family that afternoon. My mind spiralled around the logistics of what my day was *supposed* to look like before that call, strangely focused on the details of the *before*, unable to process the *now*. I was nowhere near close to the *after*.

My boyfriend called work for me and let them know I wouldn't be in, while I dressed, inexplicably, for work, and began to zombie my way towards the hospital. Dad had assured me there was no rush now, that she was receiving the best care, so to go ahead and pick up the present for my brother on my way.

It's strange looking back at it now, the things we do when we are in shock and before our minds can process what is being told to us.

On that early morning I was still willing my world to continue as if it were any other day. It was my brother's birthday and a workday. I dressed for work because it was a workday. I was picking up the present because it was my brother's birthday. Oh, and side note: then I'd be going to meet Dad at the hospital. But there was no rush, because nothing would change before I got there, because it wasn't real.

I was already in combat with the universe, engaged in a battle of wills. If I just fought hard enough, I could win.

When I arrived at the hospital after picking up the rugby ball, I was struck by the reality of the situation. The bright fluorescent lights; the lifesaving machinery beeping and pinging in a cacophony of chaos in the background; serious-looking nurses and doctors moving about with purpose. I felt like I was Alice and had tumbled down the wrong rabbit hole. I wasn't supposed to be here and, surely, neither was anyone I loved.

A lovely Irish nurse ushered me into a cubicle where Mum was lying in a bed, hooked up to all of those beeping and pinging machines. She still looked like Mum; like she was taking a nap and would open her eyes as soon as she knew I was there. It was a relief to see her looking so normal, but eerily unsettling as she remained there without moving. Not jerking awake in response to my arrival. No movement at all.

I felt awkward and uncomfortable, unsure how to address her in front of the nurse and my slightly dishevelled-looking father in the chair to the right. It felt as if I had suddenly been propelled onto the set of some hospital drama that I'd been cast in overnight.

So, I play-acted my way through the morning, listening to the medicos, talking with Dad. Doing what I did best, which was catching and unravelling every little detail, seeking that one loophole that would make all this right again, and undo the horrors of the night before. Unconsciously plea-bargaining with the universe to realise that there had been a mistake and willing the loophole to explain it all.

Later that day, Mum was transferred into Cabrini Hospital's Intensive Care Unit. The following three days stretched out in cruel agony, filled with numbness and disbelief. I found myself desperately whispering to Mum in the curtained-off cubicle, begging and willing her to open her eyes. In other moments I felt strong and stoic, trying to hold it together for friends and relatives who were visiting in droves.

We had entered a hellish limbo of waiting and hoping. Mum remained unconscious and unmoving, and I was still dressing for work. My brain was warring against the deepening reality of this gigantic, horrific, unbearable plot twist: a world without my mum. Inconceivable.

Introduction

It started to become clear, somewhere towards the third day, that we were going to have to make a decision. The highly respected neurologist Dr Jack Wodak was a lifelong friend of my father's, and we leaned on him for clarity from a medical perspective. He explained to us, in his beautifully gentle way, that based on the scans and reports he was examining, the likelihood of Mum surviving this was zero. We checked and rechecked, asked questions and overturned every stone in our minds. These conversations with Jack were what grounded me in the situation. I was somewhere between worlds: desperately struggling against reality, begging and pleading and deal-making with the universe, zig-zagging between utter distress and rationalising the information that was being presented.

But the fact was that Mum had suffered a pulmonary embolism and her brain had been denied oxygen for too long. Once we were certain that there was no hope of recovery, we made the decision to turn off the life-support machines.

One thing Mum was always clear about was that she never wanted to live in an incapacitated way. Looking back now, it's as though she had a premonition that this might be a possibility for her one day.

So, on Thursday, day three, our little family, flanked by our aunties and uncle and beautiful cousins, gathered around that hospital bed, surrounding Mum as she took her last breath.

My mind flashed back a few short days, to Monday when I was lying in bed wondering about calling Mum. An entire universe had unfolded in those three short days. What I would have given to go back for just one more conversation, one opportunity to tell her how much I loved her and what she has meant to me. But I didn't have that chance.

My mum had been the glue that held our family together; a matriarch to our extended family. She was the most important person in the world to me. And to my brother. And to just about everyone in her orbit. She was my sounding board, my advisor, my moral compass, whether I asked for her opinion or not. I would call her habitually throughout the day to chat or pass the time. I loved to make her laugh and watch the light dancing in her eyes. I wanted to make her proud and to think I was funny, or clever, or witty. She gave me the room to experiment with young adulthood, to try and to fail, and I railed against her and argued hard, even when I knew she was right. She was patient and knowing, with a quiet strength that could silence me with a single look.

She was all of those things. But she was my safe place.

Growing up, my friends and I would wake at home after a big night out, and sit with Mum to recount the night before, filling her in on the hijinks and stories, laughing until we cried. Throughout my life, she had been a friend, a stand-in parent and confidant to countless of my friends. Many of them would drop in to see her, whether I was home or not.

Introduction

She was vibrant, bold and infinitely wise, with a unique gift for connecting with people. To this day, more than twenty years later, people still tell me their stories and convey their gratitude for the deep connection they shared with my mum.

She really was special.

She was the eldest of her siblings and a pillar of strength and support to us all. The fragments began to fall away from our family foundations that day, whittling my reality into sharp perspective. Losing Mum was the first of the big plot twists in my life. Then there were others, in quick succession.

It wasn't until much later that I reflected on the myriad losses I'd experienced and realised that I really had been through a lot. More than most at that time.

But now, I've been through those life-altering moments—moments that changed the entire way I viewed and experienced the world—and have come out the other side. Those moments gave me a new language and new ways of relating to others. They connected me to an entire constellation of people who had been through similar awakenings, and this has continued to this day.

I don't have a magic formula as to how I got through it; in fact, looking back, I realise I could have supported myself much more effectively at the time, had I known what I know now. But I was young, and my priorities were all over the place.

Eventually, through the haze of grief, I became a therapist. Ironically, I threw myself into working in the deepest depths of trauma and loss, with roles in child protection, with Victims of Crime Victoria and at the Coroners Court of Victoria. Sitting microscopically close to other people's deep, ravaging grief, I felt like this was a place I could be me.

The people I worked with had a perspective on life that was familiar to me, and they helped me recognise my own grief. In the early days after losing Mum, I would have liked to know that there were hordes of people who were experiencing or had experienced what I was muddling through each day. In fact, I know now that 100 per cent of human beings will experience grief, loss and sudden unexpected plot twists in the storybook of their lives. That's every single human being on this planet.

Plot twists can take shape in our relationships, our families, our workplaces, our careers and our mental health. Our identity can take a hit; our physical health can decline. There is no part of our lives that isn't susceptible to abrupt, unwelcome transformation.

There are some walking among us who have had more than ten people's shares of grief and loss. There are others who are blissfully unaware that pivotal path deviations are just around the corner. Whether it's something you're going through now, have gone through in the past or have yet to experience, the unifying factor is that we will all endure the cataclysmic shifts of unexpected events that leave us reeling, questioning and having to reconfigure our expectations.

Introduction

It is inevitable and unavoidable.

But this doesn't need to scare us. I am living proof that we can and do survive these things and might even find ourselves taking valuable lessons from them.

If we can find a way (eventually) to see these seismic life changes as the beginning of a new chapter, rather than focusing on what we have lost or where things went wrong, we have a much better chance of opening ourselves up to new opportunities and this blossoming into a more positive mindset. One of the ways we can do that is through storytelling. The telling and retelling of our own experiences helps us to process and integrate our losses into our lives. By connecting with the stories of others and reflecting how they might differ or relate to our own, we can begin to recognise the parts of ourselves that have grown or might still need some work.

Sharing our stories is how human beings have evolved as a species through the ages. And although it might not feel like it right now, you too will evolve and grow through the hardest times in your life.

I promise you that.

1

In the Aftermath

In the early days after losing my mum I felt like I was living on a battlefield. I was fighting an invisible conflict that raged inside of me, all day and night. I was trying to rationalise my new reality; to make sense of what was happening around me and within me at the same time. I had to find ways of adjusting to my new normal: a world without my mum. That conflict forced me into maturity, making me wise beyond my years. It was an awakening to the other side of the human experience. I was stinging with a newly acquired awareness of the harshness of life, and wearing a new identity that felt completely incongruous to the old me.

And yet the world continued on around me, as if nothing had happened at all.

For me, though, every part of life had been disrupted. Everything was different. How I felt, how I thought, how I slept, which was very badly, awake for hours, plunged into the deepest parts of my feelings during those long, dark, quiet hours.

There were also new dynamics to adjust to in the rubble of our bruised little family of three. I had moved back home to stay with my dad and brother, finding comfort in being back in my old bedroom in the place that still felt so connected to Mum's presence and to the old me. We tried to claw our way into some sort of routine. My brother was in Year 12 at the time, so we had a focus: to ensure he was eating well and had the structure and support to get through the most important year of school. Really, we were all just trying to fake it till we made it.

Dad and I had never been chefs but made feeble attempts to recreate some of Mum's easier dishes. It was quite the underaking, as Mum had been famous for her gourmet-level wizardry in the kitchen. Each meal she whipped up, from the fancy dinner party to the random Tuesday night after-school dinner, catered to our various dietary requirements or preferences, and was so sublime it could have been lifted out of the pages of *Gourmet Traveller*. Unfortunately for my brother, this was not what he would come to expect for the remainder of Year 12. We fumbled around the kitchen, laughing at our incompetence, making jokes about what Mum would think or how badly we had mucked something up. But all of it was laced with the heaviness of underlying pain that was so raw, we didn't dare go near it. It was easier to joke; to run a seam of black humour through the fabric of our grief. If we stopped to acknowledge the depth of the loss, the convivial house of sticks we were rebuilding might tumble into oblivion.

We mimicked the versions of ourselves that had existed before the unbearable plot twist bent our lives out of shape. The *before* us trying to reconcile with the *after*. Although we weren't aware of it at the time, we were busying ourselves with the doing to cope with the depth of the feeling. If we had something to do, somewhere to be, a purpose through which to exist, we could keep ourselves moving forward—even when it felt like we were living in suspended animation.

I shopped for groceries for the family where Mum had always shopped. I bought the same fresh pasta from her favourite Italian shop. I trailed the ghosts of her footprints through the places that she loved, not quite ready to tread my own tracks just yet.

As well as learning to live with my own enormous sorrow, I also found myself taking on others' grief. People outside of our bubble would spend hours talking with me about their distress at Mum's death, and their loss, while I soothed and supported them. In my mind I was ranting, 'You realise I have just lost my mother, right? She was your friend, but she was my *mum*!' People shared their own stories of sadness and disbelief, as though I was a conduit to Mum and could bundle up all of their love and sorrow and pass it on to her back at home.

It was a peculiar experience, having to console the people who I imagined should have been consoling me. But grief does strange things to all of us, particularly in those early days. It can narrow our focus so intensely that it can be hard to see the impact we might be having on others. I was absorbing others' grief while only privately releasing my own. When I was alone I would cry and howl, and allow my searing pain to surface. But when others were around, I would talk about my feelings and my loss in a more matter-of-fact way. It wasn't an intentional choice to hold it together in the presence of those people; it was just how I found myself responding.

There is no right or wrong way to grieve—there really isn't. But we do have to tune in to our own minds and bodies to really listen to what they need. Unconsciously, I was recalibrating every part of my being. I was learning that although I felt like I had crumbled into a mound of volcanic ash after an enormous eruption, I was much stronger than I thought. I was a survivor, and I was surviving.

When I think back on that first year without Mum, it's a dark and fuzzy mess of hazy memories with big gaps of missing time.

In the Aftermath

While I'd moved back home in the aftermath, about a month after Mum's death I found myself wanting to reclaim some of my old life again. I decided to go back to working at the bar on weekends. I continued to seek out time with my friends, desperate to feel like the person I was before all of this messiness. My boyfriend Roscoe was spending nights with me at my family home and working alongside me at the bar. We would go out after our shifts and party into the wee hours, but I would always find myself in a corner talking to someone about the experience of grief and loss at some ungodly hour. Discovering others who had been through similar experiences before me felt like finding a pot of gold at the end of a rainbow. There was immediate connection and implicit understanding, and it was such a relief to hear that others had felt exactly the same way that I was feeling. It normalised my chaotic brain space, which was still desperately scrambling to process and interpret what was happening to me.

The processing of grief in the aftermath of loss can feel incredibly isolating. Despite those 3 am connections and the support of so, so many around me, I felt alone. I still felt the urge to pick up the phone and ring Mum whenever anything happened. Then I'd be struck by the instant snapback of truth that I couldn't do that anymore. I would wake up each morning after a few hours of cobbled-together half-sleep, groggy from the valerian or the sleeping pill that had done nothing until the morning. Before

I even opened my eyes, the crushing weight of my new life without Mum would press down on my fragile body, pummelling and bruising me again, to limp my way through another day. These heartbreaks would happen over and over again. My dreams were fraught with relentless attempts to rewrite my reality. I never felt rested. I never felt nourished.

The pain was always there, a constant throbbing of sorrow that could not be assuaged. Perhaps that's a measure of how deeply I loved my mother and how important she was in my life. But those feelings were layered with so many others: sadness for the old me whose joyous early chapters had been slammed closed; grief for the current me who was living in anguish with daily reminders of what was missing. There was also a quiet under-current of melancholy for the future me, who I could barely dare to face, knowing that I still had an entire lifetime to live without my mum by my side.

In the beginning, I was also angry. I felt robbed. Just about everyone I have spoken to who has lost someone they love through death, illness or relationship breakdown has recounted that the underlying feeling in the beginning is anger at the unjustness of it all.

I made it through the immediate aftermath, with love and support around me, because ultimately there was no alternative. The only direction was forward, dragging my pain and my past behind me.

There were a few things that could have helped me through, if I'd had the insight at the time: simple things that don't seem like much at face value, but when you add them all together they can make a real difference to how you cope with your new reality after a life-changing event.

In the early days, it's all about going back to basics: finding your way into a routine that ensures you are nourishing yourself from the inside. Taking care of yourself may be the last thing in the world that you feel like doing. You might be self-sabotaging with reckless behaviour and overindulgence in things that dull your pain, even for the briefest of moments. Food might be the furthest thing from your mind. Sleep? Forget it. Exercise? No chance.

Facing that dark abyss of grief can be incredibly confronting. Even more so is having to dive deep inside it to work out exactly what it is you need to get through.

Perhaps as you're reading this you're in the eye of that particular storm, encased in the thickness of your own distress. If this is happening for you right now, I am so sorry. It is so, so hard. But every new habit or routine begins with a single step forward. Routine is what you can hold on to while the emotions rage within you and the uncertainty rails against you. It can stabilise you until the turmoil finally abates—and, I promise you, it *will* absolutely abate. You *will* find your way through this, and you *will* feel okay again. It takes time, tenderness and understanding.

I didn't magically sail through that first year of loss and pop out the other side feeling good again. I threw myself into my social life and prioritised drinking and partying with my friends over things that may have been more helpful for my mental health. I didn't focus much on healing; I was just trying to make it through another day. Perhaps it was immaturity, given I was only 21, but in the throes of survival mode I wasn't thinking about routines or wellbeing at all.

These days I know that moving my body is important. I know that talking about how I'm feeling and digging deeper into my experience is important. I know that burying my pain and masking it with a bright social outlook will only take me so far. If I could go back in time, perhaps I would do things differently, but hindsight is tricky like that. You only know what you know at the time. And in those early days and years of grief, I was getting through it with the limited tools I had—and it wasn't all bad.

Grief and loss and upheaval take a massive toll on our physical and mental wellbeing. Our brains go into overdrive and can spiral out of control as our systems are flooded with cortisol, the stress hormone. We react with the fight, flight or freeze response and endure a neurological beating as we try to solve the unsolvable.

While our brains are hard at work, we have to fuel them. Food, sleep, exercise: in micro doses if need be. Prioritising these things gives our brains and bodies the energy they need to perform the background tasks of processing and integrating. It provides a foundation to ensure our basic needs are met. This might sound like the simplest of self-care strategies, but in the immediate aftermath, food, sleep and exercise are the things that so often fall away.

When it's too hard to manage it on your own, food can be a task you delegate to the friends and family members who might be offering to help. It's one less thing for you to think about. When somebody asks you what they can do, or what you need, food is a great answer.

Exercise doesn't have to be onerous; it can be a short walk around the block or some gentle stretching at home. Building in some movement into your day, at a set time each day, is just about making a commitment to your wellbeing even when you don't feel like doing it. You'll give yourself a small hit of dopamine and serotonin (the feel-good chemicals). It won't make a drastic difference in the landscape of your distress, but movement gives your brain a brief reprieve from all the hard work it's doing just to survive the chaos.

Sleep is the third pillar of the basic needs foundation. It helps keep the system going. Even if sleep feels chaotic or impossible to reach, it's important to try to set the tone. Give your brain the signal that you're ready to shut down. Going to bed around the same time each night is a good start. You can also implement good sleep hygiene habits such as reducing screen time in the hours before bed, dimming the lights and not having your phone near your bed. Finding other ways to unwind before bed, rather than doomscrolling, makes a big difference. Exercising during the day will also improve your chances of a better sleep at night.

In addition to good sleep hygiene and routines, there is no shame in needing some pharmaceutical assistance to get to sleep. I found natural remedies such as valerian barely touched the sides in the early days of grief, but a prescription from my GP for a benzodiazepine did help: it ensured that, for at least a few hours, I was actually getting some rest. Now, though, I'm a big advocate of melatonin, which is the body's natural sleep–wake hormone. When taken at night, it can signal to the body that it's time for sleep and put you into a restful state. All of these things should be discussed with your doctor, of course, but don't be afraid to have that conversation. Have *all* the conversations. Engage a grief counsellor or find a professional that you connect with to share some of the burden. Have massages to work out the toxins that build up in that grief state. My first massage, just a month or so after losing Mum, was gifted to me by a friend. It was absolutely brutal—just so incredibly painful. But my body needed help to release some of the heavy-duty tension it was storing in the fibres of my muscles.

So often, we find ourselves pushing through the worst of life without seeking support. But that support is there for a reason—whether it's medical support, wellness support or psychological support. If you are feeling like you're unable to sleep or unable to cope, I hope that you will reach out for help.

My mantra through my own grief—and even now, when things get tough—is *just do whatever works for you.* Resist the urge to compare yourself to others. Each of our journeys through loss, distress and change will be different. Even if your circumstances are the same as someone else's, you will go through it in your own way. Siblings will experience the loss of a parent completely differently. Friends will experience a friendship loss differently. Partners will have very different ways of responding to a breakup. We are all beautifully unique and come with our very own tapestry of childhood and past experiences that will inform the way we respond to these situations when they occur.

We know that comparison is the thief of joy. We don't need more reasons to make ourselves feel bad, pile on the guilt or worsen the negative self-talk. No one else can set the benchmark for our own recovery process. It is entirely and utterly unique to us.

What *can* be incredibly powerful is the sharing of stories. There is comfort and validation in knowing others have walked this treacherous path before us, and this is a key part of healing. But comparing and berating ourselves for feeling or behaving differently to others is not.

When you're feeling like you've stumbled down that rabbit hole of grief again, release yourself from any expectations around what the process of moving through it 'should' look like. Resign yourself to the unpredictability, and remind yourself that your grief will change shape and depth and meaning over the days, weeks, months and years to come. Knowing that you will experience sharp turns and steep drops, that your emotions will plateau and peak, is part of the process of letting go of those unhelpful expectations. The only expectation you should have is to expect the unexpected.

While you're at it, practise being kind to yourself. When you find yourself suffering more intensely than expected or reacting in a surprising way, those are the moments to say, 'Ah, this is just the next shift in my experience as I process and integrate this loss.' (That's a more sophisticated way of saying, 'Ah, grief again. Brilliant.')

Be tender with that part of yourself that is still fighting with the darkness and trying to make sense of what has happened. When life is moving forward—when you have returned to work or started a new relationship, or even found yourself laughing joyously in a spontaneous moment—you might be slapped right back into your feelings with a stinging reminder that everything is actually *not* okay, despite this moment in time. Cue the guilt, grief or anxiety symptoms.

A friend of mine had been through a difficult breakup, and had done the work in therapy and had some healthy time on her own before starting a new relationship. One night over a wine, she confided in me that she was still hurting over the end of her previous relationship and felt terribly guilty for even having those thoughts. She was genuinely happy to have found her new partner and they were at the beginning of something quite special. It felt like she had found her forever person. But there was still that little part of her that was hurting over the messy and complicated breakup she had been through with her ex. In her mind, she wasn't allowed to be feeling like that—or even be thinking about him at all.

But two things can be true at the same time. You can be happy and newly in love with someone while also still grieving a previous relationship. That grief doesn't take anything away from the new relationship and it doesn't mean you aren't 'over' your past. It simply means that you are a functioning human being with a breadth of emotional experiences that can't be compartmentalised. It's the same after a death or any significant loss. It can be extremely confronting to feel a sense of happiness seeping back in through the edges again. It can feel incongruent to the magnitude of the loss.

But after a pivotal plot twist it's important to feel joy again. Know that you *will* feel joy again. You will form new relationships and make new connections. Life will move forward, whether it's invited or not. It can be scary, daunting, uncomfortable and exciting, and a million other shades of good and bad. You might not be feeling the loss every day, or even be aware of it at all; then something might trigger a memory or a thought that brings those feelings to the surface again. And all of that is okay.

Giving yourself permission to be flawed and fluid with your emotions is a big part of the healing process. It's like the Japanese concept of wabi-sabi, which celebrates the beauty of imperfection. Learning to embrace your own emotional and reactive imperfections is one of the ways you can practise acceptance and give yourself permission to grow and flourish in spite of the pain you have experienced.

The early days are so hard. There is just no way around that. There is nothing that anyone can say to make it feel better. There is no quick fix to bypass the stickiness of all those overwhelming feelings. But tuning in to yourself and treading carefully with kindness is key. Self-care is vital, and taking it one day at a time is the only way forward.

THINGS TO CONSIDER

➤ *You are in survival mode. Your only task is to keep the basics going, even when you might not feel like it. Prioritise food, sleep and exercise, and outsource what you can.*

➤ *Ask yourself: Are there routines I could implement to support myself through this time?*

In the Aftermath

➤ *Re-evaluate any expectations you might have inadvertently set for yourself in the aftermath of your own plot twist.*

➤ *Reframe your experience and add in some kinder, more supportive self-talk. You are getting through another day and that's all you need to focus on right now.*

➤ *It's one day at a time, at this stage. One moment, one hour, one day.*

2

Treading Water

After crawling through the initial shock and the early adjustments to your new normal after a plot twist, you might be wondering, 'What next?' Which is almost impossible to answer, unfortunately. What comes next will look different for each of us and the timeline will depend on the circumstances.

Generally, though, after that acute period of grief or distress we move into what is more like a maintenance phase. In this phase, we've done the hard yards of regaining some semblance of equilibrium and may have gingerly put our toe back into the waters of the turning world. A very common theme of the maintenance phase is actually avoidance. When we haven't fully dealt with the big change we've experienced yet but life is continuing on around us, we often have to step back into the fray. We've come out the other side of that immediate aftermath and are going through the motions. Maybe you've returned to work following a death or have resumed what feels like a more predictable daily routine. Perhaps you've started looking for new work after being fired, or have re-entered the dating world after a catastrophic breakup. It might mean slowly beginning to try for a baby again after a loss, or starting, in any other way, to open up to the possibility of a future that looks different to the one you had imagined.

Integrating our difficult new reality with the world that has continued to spin around us can be a challenge—and often we fall back on coping mechanisms that aren't always the healthiest. It makes sense that we might compartmentalise our grief or uncertainty or heartache and simply get on with it, throwing ourselves into work, having that extra bottle of wine or seeking out new relationships where we can reinvent ourselves. These avoidance tactics can be effective in the short-term, but long-term growth through a plot twist usually requires us to do the 'work'.

In the earlier phases of my grief I decided to take life a little bit more seriously. In the first year without Mum, I enrolled to study psychology and hit the ground running in my career. Mum had been a psychologist herself, and it was something I thought I would eventually end up doing once all the good times had dried up. My frivolous life had come to a crashing halt in the wake of Mum's death, so I decided to fast track that aspect of my imagined future since nothing else was going the way I had planned.

Having a wealth of lived experience in the plot twist game gave me a secret superpower in the world of grief and trauma, because I truly *got it*. My superpower was really my post-traumatic growth, which gave me a greater level of self-awareness, strength and empathy. Not exactly a fair trade, but a welcome side-effect nonetheless.

After a traumatic loss or an enormous grief, we find ourselves much more aware of the vulnerability of life and what that can mean for us all. The post-traumatic growth that we experience accounts for all the ways in which we have changed after going through an enormous life shift. We might have re-evaluated our relationships or our boundaries, our limits and what we will accept in our own lives. We can connect with others in a deeper and more meaningful way, as we have a keen understanding of the recovery process that we are probably still in. Most importantly, we have become acutely aware of the resilience we have within us: our ability to cope with the horrific things that life can serve up to us.

In the maintenance phase of my own grief, I found myself drawn to professional roles that put me right in the centre of extreme levels of grief and trauma. My lived experience and recent awakening to the other side of grief fortified my belief that I had more to offer than just my professional training. I could relate to my clients on a much more personal level and that gave me a unique perspective, which I hoped would enable me to help others through their own horrors.

In that naively green way, I felt somewhat invincible. I had already survived my own big losses—well, I was in the process of surviving them, at least—and I thought I could handle anything. By the time I'd finished uni and started to work in the field, not only had I lost Mum, but several close relatives had passed away and my de-facto relationship had fallen apart. I felt I was becoming a bit of an expert in grief at that point. But, actually, I was avoiding my own grief by becoming consumed with others'.

In 2009, I was working at the Coroners Court of Victoria, supporting families in the aftermath of the Black Saturday bushfires. That work was deeply rewarding but incredibly harrowing. It tested my resilience more than any of the trauma work I'd done before it.

When I started working with families who had been affected, many had loved ones who were still missing and they were understandably desperate for answers. It was like entering a warzone. Makeshift mortuaries had been erected to handle the enormous task of receiving bodies from all of the fire zones across the state. Specialist forensic teams were working around the clock to make identifications. In our team of urgently assembled counsellors, we were receiving information and enquiries from frantic family members in the depths of intense shock and trauma. I have visceral memories of that time. The senseless devastation has stayed with me on a cellular level.

At the time, I didn't realise the toll it was taking alongside my own fresh wounds. Yet I found myself having repetitive nightmares about a desperate scramble to escape unseen threats. Dreams of smoke and fires, filled with anguish and panic. They were relentless. But this was par for the course, I thought. My naivety in the trenches of trauma work meant that I didn't really understand the impact of vicarious trauma, so I thought my experience was completely typical of the trade.

'And that's when I wake up,' I told Dr Rob Gordon, one of Australia's most revered and highly respected trauma therapists. He was sitting in a chair to my left, where my clients would usually sit, in a small counselling room at work. Dr Gordon had been called in to support the staff who were working with the victims and families of the Black Saturday bushfires.

'It sounds to me like you're trying to change the outcome for the people who have died,' said Dr Gordon. He steepled his fingers together as he peered at me through his glasses, his kind eyes hinting at a knowing smile. There was a small explosion in my brain as I took in what he had just said. I hadn't for a moment considered that perhaps my dreams were about trying to change the ending for the people who had died in those terrible, unprecedented fires. Naturally, I had thought they were about me. Trying to rewrite the story of terrible things had become a dreamscape I was familiar with.

Working with Dr Gordon was the first time I had been allowed the space to sit with my thoughts and unpack some of the impact of the work in a safe way. Prior to this, my go-to for managing the ongoing exposure to countless others' pain and distress was smashing down several bottles of wine with my colleagues and just getting on with another day, another week, another month of unspeakable grief and tragedy. The impact was huge, though I know that it was just a fraction of what the families and friends we were working with had been through.

Working so intensively with these incredibly brave people, knowing their tragedies inside and out, put me in a position where I was too close to process what I was feeling. I had leapt out of the frypan of my own grief and literally into the fire of other people's.

Subconsciously, a distraction from my own grief might have been exactly what I needed: somewhere to channel all of that angsty energy and transform it into something good. It helped me feel as though I was moving forward through the mainte-nance phase of my grief. It was an objective interruption to the mess of my own feelings at the time.

And it was the perfect breeding ground for burnout.

The years of working so closely with other people's grief and trauma, without focused supervision for much of it, led to me starting to feel the effects of the pain in other ways. I was chronically unwell with sinus infections, always traipsing back to the GP for antibiotics and follow-ups, constantly feeling run-down and blocked up. I saw an ear, nose and throat specialist and had a CT scan; I did allergy testing and started dustmite desensitisation injections; I trialled natural remedies and neti pots. I tried everything to shake the endless periods of persistent infection that kept knocking me to the ground.

One year, towards the end of my time at the Coroners Court, I was involved in supporting the family and witnesses of a high-profile case through a lengthy and very public inquest. I woke up one morning feeling a strange sort of numbness in my forearm. I thought it was unusual and mentioned it to my dad. The strange feeling continued throughout the day and into the next day. I was busy focusing on the needs of the family and witnesses, acting as a liaison between the court and the people involved, ensuring that everyone was prepared for each day ahead. There was a lot to do: emails, phone calls, preparing the young people involved for the emotionally gruelling questioning they were going to be subjected to, and managing the family's requests. There was also my other coronial work to balance, including a particularly sticky complaint I was managing, as well as my other clients' needs to meet.

The odd feeling in my arm continued for a few more days and I was starting to worry. Masking anxiety had become a daily ordeal. Sitting in court one day, next to our CEO and just behind the very distressed family, I started thinking about my arm. I suddenly noticed that it was tingling as well as numb, and realised that it was my left arm. My brain leapt to the immediate conclusion that I must be having a coronary event. Wasn't a strange feeling in the left arm usually related to heart issues? I felt a wave of panic wash over me. I started to worry that perhaps this strange-feeling arm signified more than just having slept in an odd position. A thousand thoughts attacked me at once as a rush of imagined pathology reports came flooding into my brain. Could it be this? Is it that? Hyperaware of where I was, I tried to distract myself from the anxiety. I started shifting in my seat, trying to bring myself back into the present moment and remembering why I was there. The CEO started to notice my discomfort and asked if I was okay. I nodded anxiously and gave a polite smile to a witness who was sitting nearby, who had also noticed my uneasiness.

During a break, the CEO and I rushed back to the office to catch up on some other work before we were needed back at court. I told her that I was freaking out about my arm a little bit and that I was worried I was having a heart attack or some other cardiac event. Seeing my anxiety rising, she spoke calmly with me and helped me get back into my body. She suggested that it wouldn't hurt to get it checked out, but that based on what I was describing she wasn't particularly worried.

I did go and follow it up, with both my GP and with Dr Jack Wodak, the highly respected neurologist who had been so crucial to our family's experience in those days in the ICU with Mum.

As expected it was nothing serious, but the evidence was starting to pile up: chronic bouts of illness, nightmares and poor sleep, an overwhelming level of stress that my body was starting to have physical reactions to, spiralling anxiety. It was all beginning to sound a lot like burnout.

Still, I did nothing about it. I loved the work that I was doing; I felt useful and challenged and that it was meaningful in so many ways. So, I didn't slow down.

In the years following my mother's death, I worked with victims of torture, family violence, child abuse and neglect, and sudden and unexpected death. Each of those roles rewired the way I looked at the world. Child protection made me rethink everything. The men in my life had always been beloved to me. They were kind, loving, involved, successful people. Unfortunately, the relentless work that I was doing made me jaded and I began to question every man working in a role that placed them close to children. I second-guessed crossing guards, childcare workers, shopping-centre Santas and swimming teachers. I side-eyed fathers showing genuine affection to their children. What I was seeing through my work slowly infiltrated every aspect of my life.

On the flipside, I cherished time with the children in my life: my cousin's and a family friend's babies. I spent a lot of time with them, drinking in their innocence and feeling myself swell with pride and fill with love for them, in their incredibly lucky lives.

To this day, I remain hypervigilant about child safety and over-think everything. I have plenty of hangovers from the Coroners Court, too, which has gifted me long-term anxiety about my own health, life and death.

I hadn't expected the work to change my outlook on life and the world around me so dramatically. But throughout those years of my early career, I was constantly recalibrating and adapting to new norms. It was as though the loss of my mother had shot me forward into a new trajectory that was reinforced by each subsequent loss or plot twist. In some ways, it felt like I was using my own grief for good, that there was a purpose for all of that pain and distress. 'Supportive therapist' felt much more productive than 'grieving daughter'.

I formed tight bonds with my teammates in a way that you do in trauma work. I don't remember anyone complaining about the long hours, the intensity of the work, or the jagged splinters that were left inside each of us from the grief and trauma we were experiencing, either directly or vicariously. We were all operating on adrenaline and copious amounts of cheap caffeine and sugar. Not to mention the wine.

It's a slippery slope, turning to quick fixes that mask what is really going on beneath the surface. Caffeine and sugar to replace sleep; alcohol and other substances to fill the void and muffle the trauma, personal or vicarious. The highs of a big weekend to drown out the noise of the work. None of these are healthy choices, but all were things I was doing to balance the inner turmoil of my own cumulative losses and the impact of the work I was involved with every day. All of these things probably contributed to my increasing anxiety, ongoing illnesses and poor sleep quality. Although they felt great in the moment and helped me forget some of the pain of my reality for a time, they were not long-term solutions, nor were they doing me any favours.

The connection with my colleagues and managers was crucial to surviving the intensity of those roles. I was incredibly fortunate to have extraordinary women in my life at that time. My managers in both child protection and at the Coroners Court, Liza and Michelle respectively, were the purest of gold. Wise, salt of the earth, brilliant women who provided a perfect balance of nurture, support and leading by example. They breathed a lightness into the work that was vital to maintaining our mental health. Michelle and I had a particularly special connection. She stepped in not only as a friend, but also provided the maternal nourishment that was so desperately missing from my life at that time.

Those meaningful and profound connections smoothed the edges of the parallel life I was living, with the trauma and loss in my professional life, and the losses I had experienced in my personal life. When we go through immense pain, loss, trauma, sudden change or irreparable damage, it's human connection that gets us through to the other side. And there is always the other side.

Having people to walk you through those dark days is a huge part of moving forward.

It took nine months for Dr Rob Gordon to be gifted to us at the Coroners Court. Nine months of working on the frontline of unprecedented trauma in Victoria, before we sat down with an expert to untangle some of it. As professionals who had not had a moment to come up for air and think about our own mental health, we were forced to stop what we were doing, put the files and phones down, and reflect on the impact the work was having on our own lives.

Working in the court, we were confronted with graphic photos and autopsy reports describing every detail of a person's untimely death, and were exposed to the shock and grief of loved ones left behind. Having 45 minutes to sit with Dr Gordon and unpack some of that was truly a godsend.

Ironically, the therapist in me had completely forgotten about the importance of therapy. I had mentors who had been at the coalface long before I came along; they gave unflinching advice, unwavering support and knew exactly how to quiet an anxious mind while confronted daily with the most harrowing and distressing stories. We had constant informal supervision among ourselves, and supervision with Michelle, our manager, but having access to someone completely removed from the situation, with the highest level of expertise on trauma and the brain, was an extraordinary opportunity.

Therapy and connection were the salves that kept me going. Outside of work I had deep female friendships, which are imperative for any stage of life—especially when things are taking a drastic turn. I had teammates and friends, comrades in the trenches. And having the opportunity to dissect and debrief my own personal experience in a way that you can only do with someone outside of the situation was a revelation. It shouldn't have been a surprise to learn how closely my own experiences of loss and grief were linked to the psychological responses I was having. But again, I was too close to it to see it for myself.

In my professional life, I was confident and assured. In my personal life, the landscape kept changing around me. As I fumbled through my twenties our family dynamics were shifting: there were new relationships, separations, more deaths and funerals. I was trying to balance a serious career and sombre life events with a wild and reckless private life—sometimes without success.

I was going out several times a week: casual after-work drinks with colleagues plus a big Friday night blowout and often the same again on Saturday night. I justified my hankering for a drink by the fact that everyone else seemed to be chasing that life, too. Drinking seemed to be a socially acceptable way to debrief and blow off steam after doing such heavy work. I'm not the first person in the world to treat their symptoms of burnout, stress and emotional distress with alcohol, and because so many of my colleagues were in the bars with me, it felt like an appropriate response. I was chasing the high that comes with those pleasure-seeking and risk-taking behaviours—the dopamine hit—after feeling so frazzled and run-down all the time. Outside of work I didn't have any real responsibilities at that point—no partner, no children—so I was always ready to 'pop in for one' when a colleague suggested it.

Research suggests that the separation experienced in grief actually causes a depletion of dopamine in the brain. Dopamine is the neurotransmitter associated with the brain's pleasure and reward centre. So it makes sense that we would seek to replace the missing dopamine to mute the yearning of loss. But replenishing dopamine with things that give us an instant hit but may not be particularly healthy—such as food, alcohol or other pleasure-inducing things—is definitely not a long-term solution to the pain.

It's all part of the dance we do in the maintenance phase after loss. It's a time to recalibrate and relearn about ourselves and the world, all while treading water in the uncertain ocean we find ourselves in. I wasn't in the peak of my grief anymore, but I was far from through to the other side. There were times when it felt like I just couldn't catch my breath. Pandora's box had opened after Mum died and one bad thing after another came tumbling out, each unleashing its particular kind of madness on me. I almost became resigned to the fact that bad things would happen, my life path would continue to change and nothing would stay the same. I was treading water, swimming in circles and trying to survive the dark, choppy waves.

Do yourself a favour, and don't wait as long as I did to get into therapy. I wish I had come to it much earlier in the process, rather than spending so many years in the maintenance phase. There are so many ways to enrich your experience and lessen the sting of your distress. Being a martyr only compounds the pain. Connection adds new meaning and light to your life, while therapy allows others to carry some of your burden, at least for a while.

It can be exhausting trying to keep it together all the time. Seeking help to honour the loss, and the future that may look different than you planned, is an important part of the healing process.

THINGS TO CONSIDER

➤ *How would you describe your level of burnout? Are you using unhealthy methods of coping to deal with your pain?*

➤ *Ask yourself: How can I connect with my feelings in a more meaningful way?*

➤ *Set aside time to grieve. Give yourself permission to fall apart and let it all out. Listen to sad music, look at photographs or read old messages: whatever it is that will bring the emotion out of you. Allow yourself to feel whatever comes up; it could be a whole range of emotions. Acknowledge them, write about them, name them for yourself. Identifying feelings helps you to know where to channel your energy—whether you're feeling sad, lonely, angry, resentful or a sense of longing. Identifying what is sitting beneath the umbrella feeling of loss helps to integrate that loss more completely.*

3

Filling the Void

Shades of denial, avoidance and compartmentalising the things that feel too big to process are normal following a big and unexpected change. These are your protective mechanisms in full swing. You might feel profoundly sad or be surprised by swings in your mood that haven't occurred before. Once the shock of the initial loss has worn off, the rawness of the pain can reverberate even more loudly than before.

As I've explained, sometimes the simplest way forward is to avoid our pain and seek distraction in excess—such as with work, food or alcohol. We're keen to get our mitts on any kind of distraction, and fair enough, too. For some of us, this phase is less about avoidance and more about filling the void that has suddenly opened in our lives. This can be a positive act, and we might not even realise we're doing it. Sometimes we discover something that fills our life with a new focus, allowing us the space to get a bit further along in the maintenance phase. In my case, that void was filled by Elvis Presley.

My obsession with Elvis began before I lost my mother, but it intensified after her death. In the summer after I finished high school, I was visiting a friend whose mother was an Elvis fanatic. Lounging around with not much else to do, I picked up a book about Elvis and leafed through its contents casually. The pages opened up a window into a world I had never seen before. I was mesmerised by his story and found myself deeply absorbed in the contents of the pages, finishing the entire book in one sitting.

Over time, that curiosity snowballed into an insatiable hunger. I needed to know every single thing about the man, the deity, the icon who was Elvis Presley.

This led to a decades-long, one-eyed mission to uncover the past. I spent hours scouring the internet for rare artefacts to collect on my limited single-income budget. I bought and devoured every book ever written about him; I watched every single documentary, video, film and interview ever recorded. I unearthed every recording, outtake, live and studio rendition of every song I could find. I listened to them over and over and over. I interpreted the messages behind his melodies: the pain, the anger, the sadness, the love. I pieced together my own answers to the puzzle that was the man: his life, his beliefs, his behaviour, the myths, the misunderstandings and the misrepresentations. I could not get enough.

I even took myself off to Memphis, Tennessee, filled with excitement and armed with all the information there was to know, ready to immerse myself in Elvis's real world. I arranged to stay at the Heartbreak Hotel, right opposite his property, Graceland, so that access to the sights would be simple. I had planned to stay for a few days but after my first immersion in the Elvis-sphere, I extended the trip to over a week. I went to Graceland every single day.

The attendants working at Graceland were amused by my returning on the second day, but on the third and fourth day they greeted me like an old friend and shared stories from behind the scenes, talking in hushed voices like I was privy to exclusive information that only the EP crew knew about.

I had gained access to the inner sanctum.

I soaked it all in, and I felt his loss keenly. It was so close to the surface. The question I now ask is, *why*?

Why was Elvis so important to me? What was missing in my life at that time? What was it about Elvis that drew me in so profoundly that I would cry every time I read, watched or thought about what happened to him towards the end of his life?

Like Elvis, my mother also died suddenly and way too young. They were both incredibly vibrant, enigmatic, larger-than-life figures who actually even looked a little bit similar at times.

The sorrow that I felt about Elvis's passing (which happened five years before I was even born) was deep and intense. It was a sadness that filled me up and swallowed me whole, in the same way my mother's death did. The pain was so easy to access and so very familiar.

Was I unknowingly transferring my grief about my mum onto Elvis? It's possible.

I also wonder if my obsession with Elvis was filling a void that was achingly present after the enormous and sudden life changes that were thrown my way at that time—the loss of my mother, the end of a significant relationship and experiencing hit after hit with so many of my relatives dying in quick succession over a few short years.

I was young, lost and searching for meaning.

But while I experienced a sense of magnified grief when thinking about Elvis, I also experienced incredible joy. I felt nourished and fulfilled. My horizons expanded. I discovered an entire world of music I had never been aware of before. I'm not talking about the big Elvis hits we all know (though they are brilliant in their own way). I found great depth and meaning in his later gospel work and music from the 1970s. That music was filled with emotion and sorrow, which mirrored the losses Elvis had been experiencing at the time. Elvis also lost his mother suddenly, at a young age. He had survived a stillborn twin at birth. Towards the end of his life, he suffered a very public and incredibly painful separation from his wife and the mother of his only child. The man knew sorrow.

His music spoke to my soul and it felt like cellular relief. I had found my place to be, particularly in the confusion of my twenties when life was flying past at such a dizzying rate and I wasn't always sure which way was up. Elvis and his music became my safe place, somewhere I could drop into no matter where I was in the world, or what physical or emotional state I was in.

In my work as a therapist, I've learned that people can develop obsessions with things when they are processing or avoiding pain in their own lives. (This should have been my first clue about my Elvis fascination.) It might be about gaining control when things feel so enormously out of control. It can also be a response to anxiety or stress.

People hyperfocus on all kinds of things, from the seemingly innocuous (exhibit A: Elvis Presley) to things that are more challenging if taken to extreme (exercise and food). We can become obsessed with things that take us out of our own feelings, or we might be actively seeking the dopamine hit that comes with so many of these endeavours.

But in the case of exhibit A, or similar infatuations, it is generally a sign that something is lacking in our lives, rather than us experiencing clinical behaviours that consume us in a prohibitive way.

For me, there was no intervention required; no treatment or sharp change in patterns of thinking or behaviour. Elvis was a welcome distraction from the reality of my life at that time, as I swam around in circles in the maintenance phase of my grief. I was keeping my head above water, but very much still in the deep end.

There are always knock-on effects when we've been through loss or a sudden shift in life. It's never just one, clear issue causing us distress and disruption—there can be many, for the impact of that initial plot twist is wide. But the truth is we are all hardwired, as human beings, to cope with the challenges and tragedies that life presents us with. Most of us can do this without professional intervention. But it comes down to this: accepting that terrible things can happen or have happened; knowing that it's okay to grieve and to feel; and giving ourselves permission to continue living even while we are grieving.

Sometimes, instead of facing our pain head-on, we fill up our lives with other things that help us feel as though we're moving forward. This is part of the work in the maintenance phase: getting the hang of living while still grieving. We don't always get the balance right, but that's okay. When we notice that things are out of sync or we're burying our feelings beneath a barrage of avoidance behaviours, we can make adjustments as we need, and keep going.

Again, this swinging of the pendulum between grief and recovery, grieving and living, is a very common experience. In psychological circles it's called dual process theory: where we oscillate between the negative emotions and distress of grieving and the more positive emotions, like those we find in distractions or avoidance, or in new roles or identities. We can swing between the grieving and the living experiences continually. You might have a really rewarding workout (a distraction that's good for you and helps you feel uplifted) and then come home to read over messages from your loved one (going back into the grief again). Doing restoration-oriented tasks followed by loss-oriented tasks is a healthy way of moving forward. We can allow ourselves to be present in the activity that we're doing and the subsequent emotional experience that comes with it. Over time, we will find that we're doing more of the restoration-oriented things, more of the living—and leaning less on the loss-oriented activities.

I have seen the need to fill the void in some of my clients who were missing a loved one. Their love was so immense and their grief so great that it needed to take on a different shape to fill the enormous hole left behind. For some, their loss began a crusade to uncover every detail of what had happened to their person: to understand how it could be prevented from happening again, or to advocate for others who no longer had a voice. One mother I had been working with, Toni, started a foundation to support young people with addiction after losing her son. She threw herself into that cause completely. She created an entire community of parents and siblings who had lost an integral part of their family to addiction. She brought in experts and therapists and set up supports. She raised money, went to schools to share her story and filled all of her waking hours with this important work. All of it was driven by a need to spare other families from going through what hers had.

She laughed with me on occasion, saying, 'I'm sure I've gone mad. This isn't normal.' But what *is* normal after the devastation of losing a child in the prime of his life?

Having that focus and a tangible place to pour her energy and love into helped her to feel as though she was doing something real. Especially as, outside of that work, her entire world had been suspended. She said to me once, 'I haven't stopped loving him just because he's died. The love has to go somewhere. I feel more connected to him, through this work, like I'm doing it with him.' She had found a way to channel her loss and pain into something powerful that helped her to feel human and engaged with the world when she had lost the most important piece of hers.

Another client I worked with, Jade, lost her de facto partner suddenly. In the second year after her loss, she was ready to begin the process of moving out of their shared home to find something new for herself. She threw herself into the real estate market, going to inspections, trawling the internet for suburb profiles and seeking out off-market opportunities. The process totally consumed her.

Settling on a location, she decided to trial the area by taking a one-year lease. She found her new apartment, moved herself in and was ready for whatever came next. Then a few months later, she came back to see me. She was feeling unsettled in the new place. It just hadn't been the right choice. Luckily she had the means to consider breaking the lease. Back she went on her real estate mission. She picked up the pace, taking what she had learned the first time around and applying it to her new approach. She had renewed energy and was putting everything into the process of finding her perfect home.

She settled on a different location and found a new place. I didn't hear from her again for a while after that.

When she came back to see me about six months later, she informed me that the last property hadn't worked out for her and that she was in a new place again. She said that this one was temporary, and that she was still on the hunt for the right place. When she found it, that would make it four different properties in less than a year. It was starting to sound as if there was something else going on—something bigger than the properties not being right or the location not being perfect. It seemed to me like an avoidance, or a difficulty in settling into this next phase of her life.

I continued to see Jade on and off for a few years. Our work together was largely about integrating her loss. She appreciated having a safe space to talk about her partner when it felt like most of her friends and family members had had enough of hearing about him. For her the loss was understandably still very painful; although she had returned to work and looked busy on the outside, he was still a very big presence in her life and his absence was almost too much to bear.

In those three years or so that we were in contact, Jade moved house more times than I can remember, including a stint interstate and a return to Melbourne to find her forever home. She was deeply unsettled. Her loss had uprooted her in a metaphoric and literal sense. She felt that she couldn't talk about her loss as frequently as she might have liked to. It's quite common to feel as though our grief is a burden to others, or to feel the support ebbing away over time.

Jade filled that enormous void with escapism. By burying her feelings in apartment listings, research and deliberation over locations, she was forever chasing that feeling of stability and home that was missing from her life.

I hope that she has found it, all these years later. I really do.

Since filling up my own life with love, my love for Elvis has become nostalgic, rooted in a love of the past. I remember the intensity of our time together with the fondness I might feel over a former flame. I have been thrilled to introduce him to my children and overjoyed to see them delight in his music and performances. But it's safe to say that, for now, Elvis has found his rightful place in my heart and no longer consumes my life. He is no longer the singular focus for my misplaced grief and unrequited love, or the answer to my lost sense of meaning.

Filling the void is something that most of us do without thinking. It's a protective mechanism that steps in unconsciously to manage the absence or distress we might be in. It's all part of finding meaning in this new phase of our lives as we embark on the next chapter.

But how do we actually make meaning out of these unwanted plot twists when we're coursing through uncharted waters? For some people, it's about creating a legacy for the person they've lost. For others, it can be about living a good life in their honour. It might mean taking a professional hit and hustling hard to pivot in a new direction. It might be finding a new reason for living. The key is knowing that we can and will make meaning out of these seemingly senseless deviations—it just might take a little work, reflection and time.

In my own life, and in the lives of the people I have interviewed for my podcast episodes, there is almost no way to imagine that this awful thing could turn into something hopeful in the early days of a curveball. There's a misconception that reflecting on the positives can diminish the importance of the loss—or, on the other hand, that we can't look back with regrets because the things that happened shape who we become.

It goes without saying that, in my case, I would give anything to have my mum back in my life, alive and well, a grandmother to my children. But with the hindsight of the last twenty years behind me, I can see now where so many new paths opened up and my direction changed for the better after her death. I would still give up every one of those things in a heartbeat to bring her back, but since I don't have that kind of magic, I am choosing to see and celebrate the parts of my life that have bloomed and evolved out of my pain.

My grief has afforded me a much deeper understanding of the world and the human experience. I comprehend things on a level that I would not have before. I also share an unspoken understanding with others who have been through similar experiences, who have had to grapple with the same kinds of losses as I have experienced.

The world becomes smaller in a beautiful way when you have shared experiences. And when we've been dealt a shitty hand, knowing that there are others who have gone on to have rich and meaningful lives following tragedies and deviations can be inspiring.

The thing about grief—and all the small and big changes in our lives—is that we don't ever 'get over' them; we just learn to live with them. There isn't a finite amount of space in our hearts that can be filled with love or pain. When we lose someone or something we loved, or we grieve a future that we won't get to see play out, this is not the end of our story. Our lives will continue through the pain, through the hurt. We will continue to grow and learn, and our pain will change shape.

With time, we build new layers of life around the hurt and the pain, or the loss and the grief. Our life grows around it, like the healing of a wound. The scar remains as a reminder of what we have been through, and the cells are never quite the same.

That plot twist that has thrown us off course becomes part of our new story—a story in which we are in control of the narrative, where the next chapter begins.

Just as we know that grief has many different faces, even within our own experience, so too does recovery. And like grief, the path forward is not linear. We have to find what works for us, and scramble towards survival. In the immediate aftermath of loss, it's about doing whatever works. In the maintenance phase, we're literally just maintaining our lives, treading that water, even in the choppiest of seas.

We all have that urge within us to escape the parts of life that are painful and to fill the void with things that make us feel good. But as time moves forward, it's important to be reflective and work on our self-awareness. If things are starting to feel out of balance, it might be time to change things up again.

Try to remain in the present and not worry about what comes next. It's just one foot in front of the other, one single day at a time.

THINGS TO CONSIDER

➤ *Could there be feelings that you have been avoiding dealing with? Ask yourself honestly: What parts of my life could use a little tune-up?*

➤ *Ask yourself: Am I spending more time in loss-oriented or restoration-oriented activities?*

➤ *Keep track of how you're spending your time and energy. Examine whether there might be ways to create more balance. Take an inventory of your friendships, hobbies, routines and habits—sometimes seeing them in black and white, on paper, helps to work out what might be missing or what might need a little nudge.*

➤ *As always, don't be afraid to ask for help. Even if it feels as though your friends and family are less actively engaged in your emotional experience at this stage, most would still be grateful for the opportunity to step in again if needed. As would a therapist, of course.*

4

Doing a Geographical

A few years after losing Mum, I came home one evening to find my boyfriend, Roscoe, listing items on eBay. I was 23 and we had been living together for close to five years by that point. We had a beautiful golden retriever named Casper, and were part of the same group of friends from school. Every part of our lives was intertwined.

I noticed that he was listing his prized DVD collection and the DVD stand that he had made by hand. It seemed strange that he would be trying to sell these things that were among his most treasured items. He was listing a whole lot of other items alongside those, too. Shoes, bits and pieces. It was an unusual collection of things.

I asked him what he was doing, and he told me, 'I'm going to go overseas.'

My mind was blown. What was he on about?

His face was racked with guilt. I read between the lines. My world started spiralling. What was happening? Was he ending the relationship? I was in shock and confused, throwing pointed questions and statements at him, trying to provoke a clear answer.

He told me he planned to travel extensively across continents, giving me hazy responses to my questions about what this meant for us. He had obviously been thinking about it for a while—long enough to come up with a plan to sell his valuable items on eBay and organise a rough itinerary around the world.

He was gone within weeks.

Until that conversation, I thought we were building a life together. The house, the dog, living in each other's pockets. It wasn't a perfect relationship by any means, but there hadn't been any indication that a sudden and seismic breakup was incoming. Or even a break, or whatever he was planning with this imminent escape across the seas.

Once again, everything that had felt like solid ground melted into molten lava. There was no safe place to put my feet down. We had been together for so long that I had assumed the security of our future. We had half-joked about getting engaged with a ring he had recently given me for my birthday. We'd made big life decisions together, like choosing between a baby and a puppy. We had been travelling together. We had a history as friends before the relationship began, and I hadn't ever really thought about what would happen if we broke up.

I was genuinely blindsided.

He gave wishy-washy responses to my questions about what would happen when he returned. I held on to the tiny pieces of hope that he was breadcrumbing me with through every email and phone call from overseas, maintaining the connection but never really committing either way. But I was now completely on my own. The grief that I knew so well floated back up to the surface. The injustice of abandonment loomed large. It was the same harrowing feeling of loss that I had experienced with my mum, except that I could actually talk to this person on Skype and hold out hope for a different outcome.

It was a slow unravelling of attachment that happened over a number of years. We stayed close friends for many years afterwards, and that confused things even more.

Some years later, while I was busy filling up my life during the maintenance phase of my grief, I thought enrolling in a masters degree might be another interesting way to keep moving. I was working at the Coroners Court at the time and was able to fit my study around my work hours.

The program required me and my classmates to participate

in a weekly encounter group called Group Process. It was essentially a person-centred group therapy session facilitated by one of our tutors. The intention was to fully immerse ourselves into the experience, to let go and participate as though it were a real group therapy session.

One of the themes that emerged from the group was the idea of 'doing a geographical'. In listening to their stories, it became apparent to me that many of my classmates had made deliberate moves to take themselves out of a situation and into a new environment. For some it had been a move interstate or overseas to separate themselves from complicated relationships or emotions. Some moves allowed my classmates to finally break unhealthy patterns of behaviour or complex family dynamics. Getting themselves into another location was their way of escaping the things that had been hurting them. They had rewritten the stories of their own lives, moving themselves forward in a different direction, creating a new chapter and a new tomorrow to begin again with.

At first I thought I couldn't join the conversation as I hadn't done a major geographical to restart my life somewhere else. But then, as I began reflecting on the years since Mum's death, I realised that in fact I'd done geographicals many times. I'd planned an escape, removed myself from a painful situation and sought the freedom and space I needed to feel like myself— somewhere else.

Doing a Geographical

When my long-term de facto relationship came abruptly to an end, I found myself facing the summer alone in the house that we had shared. Before the reality of that could sink in, though, my beautiful father incredibly generously offered me a ticket out of Melbourne. Using his frequent flyer points, he was able to send me off on a five-week adventure of my own.

As a young psychology student, working part-time in my father's psychiatric practice, I didn't have much money to scrape together. A ticket to Europe would have been completely out of reach for me. On the very day he offered, my dad took me into the city to transfer his points into my name and booked a ticket to London for me, leaving in a week's time. My cousin Joel was studying at the London School of Economics and Political Science at the time and was renting a room in the student accommodation on campus. This was my plan: get out of Melbourne, land in London, escape reality. I was doing a geographical.

My home life had been decimated. Mum was gone, I had been to more funerals than all of my friends put together, and now my relationship was over. We had our dog Casper, a home and a shared friendship group that was all about to become very complicated. Thankfully my dad had the foresight and the means to get me out of there before it all became too much.

I overpacked an enormous bag filled with warm clothes and an Italian down winter coat—again, gifted to me by my very generous and thoughtful father, who reminded me that it was actually going to be freezing cold in London in January. I made vague arrangements to catch up with friends in Europe but had nothing concrete locked in, other than arriving on my cousin's doorstep. I was excited about this big unplanned trip, but also a bit apprehensive about doing it on my own. Luckily, my cousin Joel is like an older brother to me, and he was also extremely close to my mum. Arriving into his care was like coming home. I felt safe and nurtured and brave enough to face anything.

From his central London room, I was able to get around town and meet up with friends with ease. It was a perfect location to take in the sights and get swept up in the swelling crowds around Oxford and Piccadilly Circus. Confusingly, Roscoe had decided to swing by London to see me for a couple of days. We spent two days together, drinking and getting silly in London, behaving as if nothing had changed between us. Given how long we'd been together, it felt impossible to avoid falling back into those patterns of behaviour and the connection that had existed between us for all of that time. I was still confused by the blurry boundaries of the breakup, or break, or whatever it was, and his talk of a possible rekindling of the relationship when he came back from his travels. As a young, grieving person who didn't want to lose another big part of her life, I think I clung to that hope a little too hard. In hindsight, the breakup was a complete blessing—we were absolutely not meant to be together for life. But at 23, with an insurmountable recent loss to integrate already, the added wreckage of a messy breakup was too much to manage. I went into denial mode.

It was a bit of a desperate time. I was in London, trying to avoid the fact that we had broken up and everything back home had changed—yet here he was, *in* London, behaving as if nothing had changed.

Denial is a clever mind trick. Sure, it serves a purpose in preventing you from experiencing pain, buying you time to build up the strength to face reality. And it can help you get through the next part of your life without actually falling apart. But it's not really that helpful in the long run.

I knew the trip was serving a purpose. It was giving me something exciting to do, new stories for my collection, new memories and experiences—even the lonely parts. Being overseas was far better than being at home, where I would have to begin my new life as a single person, living in a big house on my own, with an uncertain future looming murkily ahead. I was doing my first geographical and although it might not have been my most successful one, it set me on the road to many more solo adventures that took me right across the world.

These geographicals gave me a freedom that I couldn't find at home. I could escape the hamster wheel of developing independence and the internal pressure of having to figure it all out on my own. Being in new surroundings where I was an 'exotic' person from another country meant I didn't have to get caught up in the details of my loss or the changing landscape of my reality. I could be the best parts of myself, without having to explain or justify or compete with myself or my friends, fighting to get to the elusive next stage of life that felt so out of reach.

In the eight years that I was single, I took myself to the States and Canada, to Thailand, to Bali (too many times to count), to Sydney (a thousand times—enjoying an eight-year protracted holiday romance with a very special man, but that's a story for another time), to Noosa, to a Victorian country spa, to the Mornington Peninsula, and to Paris for six glorious weeks. Each trip gave me something to look forward to, a sense of purpose and independence, an escape and a delicious dollop of excitement. They were short bursts of distraction with new horizons that helped me do more of the living and less of the grieving.

My geographicals didn't magically resolve my heartbreak or soothe my disappointment at my place in life. They certainly didn't bring back any of the people I had lost. But those little escapes sustained me and gave me renewed energy for whatever was coming next. Each was a soul-level reset after the latest plot twist in this unpredictable life.

That first big geographical, the escape from my pain and my circumstances, gave me plenty to work through. I had to learn how to be on my own for the first time. While I had my big cousin Joel's support when I needed it, I had been pushed out of the nest and had to make decisions for myself, by myself.

When I think about the little lost puppy I was when I came back to Australia, I want to wrap her up and protect her and acknowledge all that she went through. That time in my life was cloaked in a veil of bravado and melancholy. I reserved the melancholia for the times I was alone—usually late at night, buried into the neck of my devoted dog, Casper, who soaked up so many of those desperate tears.

But at the same time, I still experienced joy and excitement, had hope and a positive outlook. Two things can be true at once. You can be grieving a past and a future that won't come to fruition, while also making the best of life in real time.

Part of regaining an appreciation for the forward movement of life came from those geographicals. It was a way of opening myself up to the possibilities I didn't know were there. Those adventures on my own gave me opportunities for growth and development that I may not have had otherwise. Each escape from my ordinary life planted seeds of understanding, some that took years to water and flourish.

On a visit to Paris with my dad and brother some years after that first big trip to Europe, following an adventure through

Poland together, I connected with a dashing French barman and his beautiful musician friend. That barman was the reason I went back to Paris a few months later, but the music was what kept me there. Like Aladdin discovering the Cave of Wonders, I discovered Le Caveau des Oubliettes: a former medieval dungeon that hosted riveting jam sessions, sending blues and soul music deep into my bones. It set me alight. As a singer and a lifelong musician, I had a reawakening. Cajoled by my friends in the piano bar next door, I brought out my inner Édith Piaf and Janis Joplin, testing out improvised riffs and melodies that the wine had given me the courage to experiment with.

I felt completely alive.

I had a gaggle of new friends, each more talented than the next, a fresh focus and a new appreciation for the electricity that a creative life can spark.

Coming home from those six weeks of immersion in a niche cultural scene in the best city in the world, I was one-eyed about starting my own blues band. I wanted to bring a piece of Paris home with me, a promise to not let myself forget how much I loved music and to hold on to a piece of that magical time.

I kept my promise. For my 30th birthday I hired a brilliant Melbourne blues band to play. I must have manifested that band into reality because before long, they were playing in *my* blues band, Firestone and Honey, as we gigged across Melbourne.

That geographical to Paris changed my perspective and my

path. I went to Paris for a boy and came home with a renewed passion for music.

There is always an escape hatch, and even though we might be reluctant to fumble for it in the dark, it's imperative that we do. Because waiting on the other side of the disappointment or the shock or the heartbreak at home, there is always another adventure ready to begin.

I had absolutely no idea that my geographicals would spark a new energy in me in the way that they did. But because of those trips, spinning away from the tedium and disenchantment at home, I unlocked the door to the next phase of my life.

It's easy to look back with hindsight and say, 'That was the moment that things changed for me. Because of that interruption or choice that I made, or that thing that was inflicted upon me, my life went in another direction.' The tricky part is making those changes while life is happening. So, instead of waiting for something to reveal itself, we should proactively take leaps and throw ourselves into unknown situations. By seeking new opportunities and experiences, trying things out and taking risks, we're opening up windows and doors into new possibilities.

That's not to say that every heartbreak leads to something wonderful, but I do believe that every experience of pain and loss is an opportunity to learn and grow.

Someone who embodies the lemons-to-lemonade principle is the beautiful Lotte Bowser, who I had the privilege of talking with for my grief recovery podcast, *The Days That Follow*. Lotte has experienced loss and pain on an indescribable level. Just before Covid struck, Lotte's beloved partner Ben was diagnosed with a rare and aggressive form of soft-tissue sarcoma. The couple faced it together head-on, through surgery and radiation therapy, and, with sweet relief, they learned that Ben had the all-clear. In that moment they decided to seize and celebrate every moment of life together. They went travelling, got engaged and were feeling ecstatic about the future.

Three months later the pandemic swept through the world. Ben went for a scheduled follow-up appointment, where they found that the cancer had spread to his lungs. The specialist told Ben, in no uncertain terms, that he would die from this cancer. Lotte was gripped by terror. Her world that, just three months before, had begun to stabilise and thrive, was spun off its axis again.

In an instant, Lotte and Ben went from a vibrant young couple brimming with hope and fizzing with big dreams for their future, to managing a stage 4 terminal illness under the restrictions and isolation of Covid lockdowns.

Lotte launched into action. She spent night and day in a frenzy of research and investigation, trying to do everything she could to give Ben the best chance of fighting this cruel diagnosis. Nothing worked. The treatments were gruelling, with agonising results. They were all alone, just the two of them, as they fought for Ben's life and protection against outside illness.

After just a few short months, their medical team advised that they had come to the end of the road. There was nothing else they could do to prolong Ben's life.

Refusing to accept that from their UK doctors, after an exhaustive search Lotte found a cancer treatment centre in Mexico that specialised in rare cancers like Ben's. In the most dangerous city in the world. At the height of Covid.

After three or four weeks of taxing treatments, they finally had some good news. The treatment was working. Finally, they had a glimmer of hope that they might actually make it through this unbearable nightmare.

Less than a week later, they both began to feel unwell. Ben became incredibly sick. After an exceedingly traumatic time for them both, devastatingly, Ben passed away in the Covid ward of a Mexican hospital.

Lotte and Ben had both been through unimaginable highs and lows. The rug had been pulled from beneath them countless times. Then, just as quickly as they had found the tiniest shard of hope, it was cruelly ripped from their hands in the most painful way.

Every fibre of Lotte's being had been dedicated to helping Ben survive each battle. She'd been through an unrelenting onslaught of duress and distress. After losing Ben, Lotte's world became one she couldn't physically be in anymore. Every location, sound and sight became an aching reminder of what she had lost. Not that she needed reminding. It was just too much.

So, Lotte did a geographical.

She took a leap of faith and moved to Lisbon, Portugal. Everything about that change of scenery breathed new life into her and filled her with hope and possibility. Not for one moment did the move take away her pain or her loss, but it transformed her in every other way. Something that being in her old life, in London, could never have done.

In her own words, Lotte's life looks radically different now to how she thought it would. It hasn't come easily, either, but making that transition to a new physical location gave her the space to grieve and heal in a transformative way.

Being in a new environment does wonders for the soul, even after the most dire and tragic circumstances.

It's also a helpful reminder that nothing stays the same forever. Every part of our life is a chapter with a beginning, a middle and an end. It sounds scary, and there are some awful chapters that we wouldn't wish into anyone's book. But knowing that we have the ability to choose what our next chapter should look like is an empowering thought.

In Buddhism there is a concept called the law of impermanence. It is the belief that everything has a beginning, a middle and an end—from our material possessions to our relationships, jobs and the people in our lives. In fact, everything around us exists in a state of impermanence, from the smallest to the greatest things that we know and see. The plants and the trees, the buildings and the roads, our countries and the planet—everything that we know, in this lifetime, will eventually come to an end. Although impermanence can sound quite frightening in an existential way, the concept and, indeed, this chapter are not intended to cause fear or anxiety. Instead, the idea is to illustrate the point that life is perpetually in flux, and that change is an inevitable constant. It's a beautifully simple idea.

According to Buddhist principles, it is perfectly okay if this notion causes worry or concern. Reflecting on the state of impermanence within our lives does not mean we don't feel the depths of despair or the enormous injustice of losing someone we love. Instead, it is an opportunity to sink right into our emotions and allow ourselves to feel what comes up when we think about this. The sadness, the worry, the discomfort—our feelings are natural responses to the idea or reality of losing the things, people and places we love. Hiding from our emotions will only prolong our pain.

Doing a geographical is like putting a bookmark into our lives in a place we think might be a beginning, a middle or an end of one chapter. Removing ourselves from the physical space where our greatest grief lives provides food for the soul.

A recent trip to the Gold Coast gave me an opportunity to pause and recharge in a way that I haven't for years. I took myself out of the chaos of my daily demands to sit on the sand in front of the roaring ocean, staring out at an expansive horizon for four days. It gave me a cellular shift and a reset that every inch of me had been screaming out for—without me even knowing. Being able to absorb all of that fresh sea air and feel the sun on my skin filled me with renewed energy and enough gas in the tank to sustain me for a considerable time back at home.

If you're in the midst of a plot twist and someone says, 'One door closes and another one opens', or, 'Everything happens for a reason', it can be a bitter pill to swallow. Platitudes are unhelpful when you're in the thick of it. But taking yourself physically out of the space of your greatest pain can be an incredibly healing experience.

Of course, moving countries or taking an interstate trip might not always be possible, but there are other ways to break up the monotony of grief and loss and gain a fresh outlook. Spending time in a new place, immersing yourself in a national park, seeking out a sunny spot by the water or even taking yourself for a day out in the city can shift your perspective. This kind of reset can spur you on and support you in putting one foot in front of the other. Shifting your energy into a fresh location can remind you, even temporarily, that there are joys to be had and new memories to be made.

THINGS TO CONSIDER

➤ *Ask yourself: Would a geographical work for me?*

➤ *If it's been a while between breaks, could you plan a weekend away? Or an extended trip? Even a day trip does wonders for the soul. Sometimes just the planning itself gives your mind something to focus on and can be a welcome distraction.*

➤ *Could you set up a Pinterest account and start scouring the internet for aspirational getaways? Do some research into locations near home that you haven't explored yet. Ask friends if they would join you in some escape therapy and make new memories together.*

5

Identity

The plot twists in life are not reserved only for the terrible things that can happen to us, or around us. Beautiful, wonderful, joyous times can also present us with unexpected script flips that we may not have been expecting.

Like becoming a parent for the first time.

Parenthood changes you in every way: from who you are as an individual to who you are within your family and community. It might alter your career path. It can change your friendships and your outlook on life.

One minute you're a fully functioning member of society, expertly balancing a career, relationships, friendships and the world around you. Enter the baby and your house of cards tumbles into disarray, only to be reshuffled and restacked in a completely different order. Your priorities shift, your patience thins and what is most important can look completely different to before.

It's as if, with the birth of your baby, you acquire an entirely new set of personality traits, complete with overwhelming love that explodes out of every pore, coupled with overthinking, anxiety and a new sense of trepidation. All of it leaves you constantly worrying that something is wrong, that you don't know what you're doing and that every erroneous move will send you deeper into the wasteland of brain-fried uncertainty.

At least, that's how it was for me.

I was absolutely thrilled to be in the baby bubble for the first time, but I hadn't expected it to happen quite so soon. I had enjoyed an easy pregnancy full of wonder and excitement, following all the apps daily to see what changes my little growing fruit had made that week and enthralled with each development. I was looking forward to an extended break from work and being able to put my feet up and watch my shows. At that time, I was working as a therapist in a school and for an online Australian university. I wrapped up my clients and prepared to go on leave four weeks before my due date. Just a few days into my leave, though, I had a sudden urge to prepare the baby's hospital bag. I still had four weeks to go, so I wasn't overly anxious about it—it was just an instinct, to get his bag ready. I carefully washed, dried and folded his tiny little items of clothing and ensured I had enough of everything on the list provided by the hospital.

That night, after attending a family friend's seventh birthday party, I woke up to a feeling of an explosion in the bed. It was as if a water balloon had been thrown at full force and blasted me awake with its impact. The bed was wet all around me. I knew exactly what had happened and jumped out of bed.

'Chris! My waters have broken!' I called out to my partner, who had only just gone to sleep after working at an event. He looked up at me groggily as I stood beside the bed trying to work out what to do next. 'Can't you just put a towel down and come back to bed?' he asked. 'No, I can't! We need to go the hospital!' I retorted.

Neither of us fully knew what was going on. We were still just under four weeks away from the date we had *expected* to become parents. I had not packed a bag for myself, and we still hadn't organised half the things we needed for the baby as we had planned to do that in the month-long lead-up to delivery.

I called the hospital and they advised that, yes, it was time to come in. The midwife told me to pack a few things for myself and to calmly make our way in.

I rang my dad to tell him what was going on as I waddled slowly around the room, squeezing my legs together and trying to think about what I needed to bring to meet my baby for the first time. A sudden eruption of my waters was a plot twist we had not anticipated so early.

Our little one was in a hurry to get here, and we were not prepared.

When he did arrive early the next morning, he was tiny: only 2.4 kilograms and so small that we could only use two fingers on his back to burp him. The one bit of organising I had done in that intuitive nesting I did the day before his arrival turned out to be quite pointless, as he didn't fit into any of the clothes we had for him. We were able to get some premmie size 00000 baby suits from a friend who had also had an early delivery, as well as a little suit from the hospital to tide us over until we got home.

He was perfectly healthy, with everything functioning beautifully, but he just hadn't had those final weeks of cooking to put on any of the crucial baby fat that comes in the last month of gestation.

It also meant that he spent most of the first week of his life in the maternity ward nursery, having his weight and temperature constantly measured. I turned into a solo milk production factory, learning how to feed this tiny little human, then having to express on a strict 24-hour schedule to ensure that our little man was being fed at all hours and fattened up as quickly as possible. It was an enormous undertaking and one that didn't leave much time for anything else.

Identity

My whole life was now solely about the needs of this helpless little thing, and everything else faded into the background. I wouldn't have had it any other way, but it was a drastic switch from the high-achieving, always-busy, highly functional person that I had been not long before.

It's almost as though your former identity evaporates into thin air with the birth of your child. No amount of pre-planning or reading can prepare you for the enormous shift in your role, which catapults you further away from your old life with each child you add to the family.

In the early days you're numbed by fatigue and overwhelm, living in the tiny windows between feeds and sleep. The house admin becomes insurmountable. By the time all the mandatory tasks are complete, you're faced with another onslaught of things that need doing.

And sure, all of that domestic chaos is awash with the most colossal feelings of love, awe and disbelief, as you drink in the tiny little person who is suddenly very real and in your arms.

But it's a complicated time. You find yourself constantly second-guessing everything and feeling like the greenest member of your new world, learning everything on the job, checking and wondering and googling it all. It's an instantaneous transition, an undeniable identity shift.

The brilliant Georgie Abay wrote about this in her book *Best Laid Plans*, and we had a deep exchange of ideas and war stories in a conversation for my podcast, *The Curious Life*. Georgie described one particular night, at the weeping end of complete and cumulative sleep deprivation, when she found herself swearing at her tiny little baby, who just would not stop crying.

Coincidentally, I was talking with Georgie on the morning after a hideous night of my own. Our third child was just seven weeks old and had decided that the night before my interview with Georgie was the perfect night to stay up and scream uncontrollably for hours at a time. I, too, found myself in the last throes of sanity, mad with despair and pleading for respite. I, too, may have sworn at my tiny little person, pleading irrationally with him to just 'Go to sleep!' It was a revelation, knowing that Georgie (and, I'm sure, countless other parents) had also been brought to the edges of reason and rationality through the snake pit of desperation and distress. A new baby is the quickest way to get there. Especially if you plan on doing any non-baby-related tasks during waking hours.

Would either of us have ever imagined swearing at tiny, innocent babies as the previous versions of ourselves? Absolutely not. This was a plot twist side-effect.

Georgie also shared the notion that when our children are born, so too are we. Our new identity and role as a parent is birthed at the very same time. Being a mother to three young boys myself now, the plunge into chaos has never felt more real.

I have also personally never been busier, both inside and outside the home. Which, as we know, can be a recipe for disaster. I love Georgie's take on the rebirth. Rather than seeing this seismic shift in identity as a loss, how beautiful it is to see it as the beginning of something new?

During my first year of parenthood I was excited to experience it all for the first time. I wasn't entirely aware of how big the transformation within me would be.

While on parental leave I took on a few private clients who I would squeeze in between sleep and feed cycles, one of whom was a beautiful little boy referred to me by a friend and colleague. This angelic little man was just a few years older than my fresh little baby and had a bright energy that pulled me in. He was referred to me because he was in the middle of a fight for his life. That golden boy was fighting terminal cancer.

Having considerable experience working with families in grief and trauma, I felt skilled enough to work with Bailey and his family as they navigated the dark waters of uncertainty. But I hadn't given a great deal of thought to the emotional impact that taking on this referral might have on me in my very new role as a parent.

It was a stark contrast and the sharpest reality check for me, emerging from the cocoon of my baby bubble, with my healthy little slug waiting for me at home, while sitting across from the strongest woman I had known for a long time. Bailey's mum

Ananya was like something out of a movie: beautiful beyond words, elegant, refined, unpretentious with a deep warmth that emanated from her. The connection between mother and son was profound.

I first met with Ananya and Bailey when my little one was just ten weeks old. I was in my early 30s and had seen much of the world by then: all the darkness and pain, harrowing grief and loss, misery and injustice at the coalface. This work was not like that at all.

It could have been, given the distress that comes with a diagnosis like Bailey's, but Ananya enveloped him in a light and love that stretched beyond the here and now. It was desperately sad to imagine a world where he didn't get to grow up—absolutely unthinkable—but there was something so powerful about Ananya's love that it felt safe to stay in the present.

Working with Bailey to help him verbalise some of the overwhelming experiences his little mind and body had been through was a privilege. Bearing witness to motherhood on such a deep and profound level was awe-inspiring.

There was a significant contrast between my daily gripes and fumbles in new parenthood and the very real fears that Bailey's family was facing. I couldn't begin to fathom the courage and strength required to fight the illness from a medical perspective, while also maintaining the resilience and hope that was needed to keep the family buoyed and moving forward. Ananya was a warrior.

While my life and identity were undergoing a transformation into this new phase, at the opposite end of the spectrum, Ananya's were, too. Just as my life had changed overnight, so too had hers. Her role, her identity and her purpose were now entirely redefined due to an incredibly cruel and painful turn of events.

I wondered if I would be as graceful and present if I were faced with such a trial myself. I also wondered how you manage that enormous transition from everyday parent negotiating the chaos of life, to parent of a child with a life-threating illness. Almost instantly, the problems of the day would recede into the distant, yearned-for past.

This is something radio and television star Kate Langbroek knows intimately, as she shared during our chat for *The Curious Life*. Her story gave me a deeper understanding of the experience of a parent whose life is no longer their own. A parent who must pour everything they have into their child's treatment and survival—the most unfair and unjust twist of fate, which changes their life in an instant.

I asked Kate how she managed to stay strong for her beautiful boy as he underwent the painful and invasive treatments that ultimately saved his life. What was it that kept her going when the future was so unbearably bleak? She said that she did it because she had to. She had no other choice. While she had been fortunate with a blessed outcome for her son Lewis, so many families had not, and she was desperately conscious of this as we talked.

In simple terms, she described it as the power of love; that with great love comes great responsibility. She said, 'Even if you desperately wish that a UFO would come and suck you up, just to take you away from having to witness things that you should never have to see—there's a stronger force that keeps you here and keeps you going, one step in front of another, even when you think you can't. That is the power of love.'

It's often the hardest things in life that make us who we are. Sometimes it feels as though the great tragedies in our lives mark the end of our happiness, the rupturing of our dreams and our hopes for the future. This may be true, but they can also, with time, become our greatest teachers, the lessons from which we grow. I wouldn't be who I am today, have the career that I have or even be writing this book, if I hadn't been through my worst days. I learned terrible lessons about loss and resilience that have made me who I am.

While we were sharing our experiences with loss and grief, Kate asked me whether I would give up everything I had ever had with Mum to save myself from the deep, distressing grief that followed her death. Of course, the answer was (and is) no. I wouldn't trade all that love, or the years I had with my mother that shaped me as a little person, to spare myself the scars that her death left behind.

And while I would give anything to have her back, so much of my growth and learning has come from the hardships of loss. Though death and heartbreak can feel like lopping off limbs without warning, like razing an entire forest of trees to the ground, they can also lead to new leaves and tender new shoots of hope sprouting. In time, when we look back, we will see the beginnings of a new forest that have sprung up around us where the trees once stood tall.

Life will never look or feel the same as it once did, but our identity can be reborn again and again, adapting to meet us in the place that we find ourselves in.

Resilience is a truly remarkable human trait—an invisible fighting spirit that spurs us on, just when we think we can't handle even one iota more. Turns out we can. Just like Ananya and just like Kate.

There were many times when I felt it was too much and I couldn't take one more disappointment, loss, rejection or heartbreak. And in those times, it was important for me to express that and admit some kind of defeat, even momentarily. This allowed me to let go of some of the turmoil and angst that had built up. While it felt as though I had not a whisper of strength left, nor the inclination to summon any, somewhere hidden inside was a secret box with just enough of the stuff to get me back on my feet and fighting again.

During the years when I was going through all of those big upheavals, it felt like I didn't have much of a choice but to just keep going. It wasn't exactly an active decision, to put one foot in front of the other and survive every hit—it was just something that happened.

Resilience is funny like that. As a therapist and parent, I know there is a lot of focus on building resilience in kids: arming them for the future; instilling in them the vigour and vitality to face challenges when they arise with clarity and assuredness.

We all have resilience inside of us—even if we have been through trauma, had questionable parenting or didn't have the privileged, love-filled upbringing that I'm keenly aware I did. We all have the ability to move through our worst days, when the rug is pulled unexpectedly from beneath our feet and we find ourselves dazed, confused or in pain. Something deep in us knows that in spite of this unexpected shift in the plot line of life, there is hope beyond this.

Sometimes it's just holding on to that belief, like a tiny flickering flame, knowing that one day we'll be able to grow that glowing ember into a giant blaze again. We might not see the way out immediately; in fact, it almost goes without saying that at the time of the event that changes our path in life, we won't be able to see the next move very clearly at all. But just *knowing* that a path will again appear is enough to keep going.

That's what Kate Langbroek did. She just kept going. By trusting in the power of that forceful love that she felt, so wildly out of control and unfaltering, she was able to keep going.

Part of the stress of these pivotal or painful life moments is the fear of the unknown. Understanding what is at the root of our fear can help us move towards the parts of ourselves that might need some extra support or attention. Having a guide map to where our feelings come from and how they are being expressed will help us manage ourselves through those stormy seas. Sometimes even just saying what we're feeling out loud, writing it down or sharing it with another person helps to take some of the power out of the feeling and, in turn, makes it easier to control.

When we are rudderless at sea, flooded by emotion or information overload, we cling to moments of direction and find meaning in the smallest of signs. Resilience is what pushes us through, but believing that things *will* one day improve is the guiding light.

When I was a new parent, I was immersed entirely in the entanglements of responsibility and adoration. I didn't have the headspace for much else. But I didn't begrudge my new role: it was all so novel and consuming and constantly changing, with new routines and patterns to adjust to. It took up all my time and energy.

It wasn't just a shift in identity; the very fibre of my being had changed.

Two years later, when I was on parental leave with our second child, I was changed again. The leap from one child to two was a shock to the system. We were thrown into chaos once more, with no choice but to surrender to the noise and demands, abandoning all hope of a tranquil home where objects return to their rightful places each night; where we were not suffocating under masses of unfolded washing; where we were getting enough sleep to maintain brain function. Whoosh, out the window.

Strangely, though, this period of parental leave was nothing like the first one. The first pregnancy, the first leave—they were a luxury that I now wish I had savoured a bit more.

The second time around I was itching to do something, bored by the hours at home with a well-behaved baby. It was at that time that I found a desire to explore my creative side rising within me again.

In the years before kids I had done some freelance writing work on the side, writing features and travel stories and working as a contributor for a digital innovations and technology site. Thinking it might be fun to combine my skills as a therapist and as a writer, both areas where I used interviewing skills in different ways, I thought I would try to create a podcast. So, between those feeds and sleeps, I taught myself everything there was to learn about starting your own podcast. Google was my friend and I relished the new vertical learning curve. My brain felt stimulated and engaged in a way that it hadn't for a long time.

My identity changed again.

I was a mother to two boys, a therapist and a podcaster.

Adding to the madness, several years later we welcomed baby number three. There was a huge difference between having a two-year-old and a newborn and now having a six-year-old, a four-year-old and a new baby. The third time around was wild, loud and busy beyond words, but we also had the respite of child-care and school, play dates, sport and activities to keep the older ones out of the way and occupied.

My identity shifted again. A mother to three children. A mother to boys, *three* boys. I had always imagined having three kids, but never did I think I would be parenting three boys. Those who have come before me assure me that three boys is a gift that will reap rewards when they're older, but for now, it's chaos. Messy, loud (did I mention loud already?), clamouring, climbing, boundless energy chaos. The exuberant love is tremendous, suffocating at times. There are days that I can lean in to those after-dinner noise spirals and just roll with it, and other times that I am in complete and utter sensory overwhelm.

The difficulty lies in the fact that I have so many other things I want to be doing in conjunction with parenting. I have a book to write, two podcasts to host and produce, deals to negotiate, a job to fulfil, clients to see, workshops to create and run, and media responsibilities to meet. All of it is so much fun and so incredibly fulfilling from a personal and professional viewpoint. My brain feels engaged in a new and exciting way, and I'm being challenged to learn new skills and fill my head with fresh knowledge. This is something I crave.

Being pulled back from that into the needs of my family can be difficult. Then of course comes the cascade of guilt and frustration, and disappointment in my lack of patience and my inability to create separate lanes for my energy and responsibilities. My identity is constantly shifting and changing. I know this is something many parents wrestle with: trying to work out which hat to put on at which times, and how to honour the parts of ourselves that need more attention.

Some experts believe that our identity is formed in late adolescence, and that it then continues on a relatively stable path through our lives. But, like most life experiences, identity is not linear. It changes as we do, evolving and growing, taking sharp turns and subtle shifts. We toughen up when we need to or relax our boundaries and beliefs, and sometimes even find ourselves at the opposite end of the spectrum to where we first started. This flexibility to adapt to new circumstances is part of the reason we might find our new selves at odds with our old selves once our paths have been irrevocably changed.

When Georgie Abay described swearing at her little baby, desperate with sleep deprivation and the special kind of madness that only a newborn can induce, I felt seen and heard. It was an incredible gift to my own sanity; an important reminder that my landscape was changing exactly as it should be and that, instead of fighting it, I needed to lean into it.

Sitting with Ananya's experience and hearing Kate's story of resilience reminded me that we don't know the strength we have until it is put to the test. We don't know what we can survive until we have to.

Our identity can be ruptured and repaired—and rebuilt again, with every twist in the road. Resistance is futile! Who we are on the inside will continue to shift in response to our life stages, and that can be a blessing and a gift.

Some of the challenges that arise can come from that feeling of incongruence between our old life and our new life following an unexpected shift. Finding a way to accept the changes within us, without judgement and without resistance, is the quickest way forward.

There is more than enough to deal with in the aftermath of a shock—so many things for our overwrought minds and hearts to try to resolve. Scrambling to get back to who we were before can be an uphill battle. We are forever changed by these big life shifts, but that doesn't mean that one part of us dies. We are, however, different to before.

Reconciling the old version of ourselves with the new can be challenging. But if we shift our mindset from the change being negative and another thing to grieve, to understanding that shifting identity is part of the process of change, we might find we are more at peace.

The bottom line is that we can't go back to who we were before. It's just not possible. The version of us who was naive to pain, grief or loss just doesn't exist anymore. If we identify the things that have changed and outline what we have learned in the process, this chasm between the old and new versions of ourselves may begin to stitch together. This is part of that post-traumatic growth; it enables us to acknowledge the things that have changed for the better—as difficult as the circumstances were that led there—*after* we have experienced great pain or loss.

Resenting the difference in ourselves will only make it harder to move forward. The new version of ourselves—a stronger, more resilient, more capable person with a plethora of new coping skills—is something worth celebrating.

THINGS TO CONSIDER

➤ *Acknowledge the new you with kindness and empathy.*

➤ *Ask yourself: What lies beneath the surface that may be causing some resistance to the new me? Is it fear of change? Fear of death? Fear of being alone?*

➤ *Write out a list of all of the things that have changed in the time post–plot twist. Notice the smallest shifts in your outlook and responses. Are you braver or more vocal? Do you have clearer boundaries? Are you more open to new relationships and connections? Do you put yourself first now? Acknowledge and celebrate these post-loss developments. They do not detract from your loss; they only make you stronger.*

6

The Mind and Body Connection

It's so easy to lose the connection between our minds and our bodies when we lose our footing. When our plans and expectations are blown apart thanks to whatever unforeseen event dropped the grenade, all the things we know work for us can evaporate into thin air.

I don't actually remember doing any structured exercise in the first few years after Mum's death. I was young, reasonably fit and healthy, so I hadn't really needed to establish a routine around exercise at that point. I was just muddling my way through in survival mode, eating whatever I wanted, getting messy and wild with my friends and trying to ward off the worst parts of the pain without too much effort.

But I was also finding it very difficult to sleep. I was

experiencing increasing levels of anxiety and I wasn't employing a single healthy strategy for addressing my grief. At that time in my life I still hadn't made the connection between physical and mental health. In my world, exercise was just something you did to get fit.

The anxiety I was experiencing was exacerbated by the things I was seeing in my work at the Coroners Court, giving my brain more ammunition to flood my body with sensations that triggered fear and worry within me. I was hyperaware of what was happening within my body all the time.

The voiceover in my head became the outline of a police report. I was constantly imagining that whatever the niggle or strange feeling I was experiencing in my body was going to be the reason for my sudden demise right there and then.

It was exhausting.

I knew it was anxiety, but the fact that my mind could make the physical symptoms feel so real—and my lived experience so miserable—was quite astounding to me. I couldn't believe that my brain had so much power over my body. I just wished it would use its powers for good instead of evil.

I was also learning, through those years, that I did bounce back from the setbacks and the disappointments. I could move through the rejections and failures, even alongside the spirals into panic and anxiety. Sometimes I would have to sit in the feelings for a little while and give myself permission to cry it out or have a little pity party. But I was learning that those moments didn't last long. I could wallow and grieve or bemoan my current situation, but then it was time to keep things moving. Back to the dating apps, back into hobbies or interests or activities, to keep that mind of mine busy.

When I had matured a little and was going through the subsequent losses and relationship breakdowns that followed Mum's death, I found that exercise was part of what made me feel good. I would go through phases of commitment to various different things, from taekwondo and kickboxing to yoga and gym memberships that never quite stuck. But even then, I was still just doing it for my body, with a dash of feeling good about myself on the side.

It didn't really occur to me that it was my confidence that was significant. And the confidence came from the feel-good chemicals and hormones that were released through exercise.

I eventually found what worked for me, which was daily walks with my dog Casper and as much Pilates as I could reasonably fit in. At my peak I was doing up to four high-intensity reformer Pilates sessions a week. I definitely wasn't fully aware of the mental health benefits that were unfolding, but I knew I liked how it made me feel. A bit slow on the uptake, perhaps?

In recent years I haven't had the luxury of free time to attend so many classes. In fact, I've had a voucher for Pilates that has been collecting electronic dust in my inbox for a full year now because I haven't been able to carve out an hour regularly enough to make it worthwhile.

When I've thought I might have a window to start again, I have been plagued by illness or injury that has prevented me from going. I've also been suffering from extreme levels of anxiety again and I know it's a bit of a conundrum. My mental health isn't great, so I'm not motivated to exercise. But because I'm not exercising, my mental health isn't great! This often happens both in the immediate aftermath of a giant plot twist, and at any other time in life when things begin to feel a bit overwhelming. I talk about this connection between mind and body all the time with my clients, yet it's something I'm not always great at following through with myself.

On a recent walk with a dear friend and colleague we were talking about the premise of this book, and she dove into what has helped her move through the unexpected moments in her life. When she was 40, Wendy experienced a series of events that upended everything she thought she could rely on. She had just moved interstate to take on a new role in advertising. She had carefully carved out her life path and it was beginning to take shape. She was brimming with excitement on the precipice of her new life. The move to Melbourne marked an enlivening new chapter in the book of Wendy in Advertising.

Three months into her new role, Wendy was involved in a major car collision that briefly left her unable to see clearly and with a terrible whiplash injury. This was absolutely *not* in her plan for the beginning of her new life.

Waking up the day after the accident, Wendy knew her body was in shock and recovering from the impact of the crash. Completely committed to her new role, though, she was determined to make it back to work asap. Not even a serious road accident could stop her. The very next day, with cloudy vision and unable to even make out the street signs, Wendy diligently made her way to work. Within a day or two her vision was restored, but she was left with an undiagnosed neck injury that slowly began to make itself known.

A short time later, just as quickly as it began, the dream job in Melbourne dissolved when the client she had been hired to manage pulled out of the contract. In an instant, Wendy's new life vanished. Without the client, there was no role. Wendy was retrenched.

There she was, having just uprooted her life to move to a new state, suffering a sudden and unexpected injury and now out of a job. It was a trifecta of challenging circumstances that occurred in quick succession. Wendy had thought her life was mapped out ahead of her, but the universe had other plans. With rent and bills to pay, her future uncertain and her body needing time to recover, she was in a frightening predicament.

Losing your job shortly after leaving your home state and being involved in an accident that causes ongoing injury and pain would be a compelling reason to believe that the universe was conspiring against you. It wouldn't be unusual to spiral into negative thinking, to slip into depression or anxiety or to have a visceral cortisol response that might force you into fight, flight or freeze mode. The stress and pressure would be immense. Do you madly race back into another corporate role to keep the career trajectory blazing forward? Do you pack up your things and move back home, over the border, to start again? Do you bury your head in the sand and try to avoid having to make any decisions at all?

For Wendy, the solution came in stages. First, it was establishing the connection between her physical health and her mental health that moved her forward. Having the neck injury gave her an immediate focus. She resumed yoga and physiotherapy and gave her full attention to her physical wellbeing. She soon discovered the infinite benefits to her wellbeing and mental health. That focus on her recovery and the time away from the corporate world gave her the space to listen to her body's needs and enjoy the rewards that the mind and body connection can bring.

That's when things began to shift for Wendy and a new path began to materialise in front of her. She had always wanted to study psychology or therapy in some form but had never been able to find the time to squeeze further study into her busy schedule or demanding work roles. Being injured, retrenched and freed up from obligations gave her the space to explore the ideas that were bubbling away inside her.

To address the sudden lack of employment, she took a leap of faith and began freelancing. This opened up an entire world of possibilities and allowed her the time to finally enrol in the course of study she had long been dreaming of. This would never have been possible as a senior in advertising, working long hours that left little room for anything else.

The life-changing events that could have been catastrophically disruptive to her life are the reason that Wendy has a thriving career as a therapist today. She has well and truly left the corporate advertising world behind her and now spends her days helping countless others through their own trauma and pain. She works the hours that suit her, with complete freedom and flexibility to immerse herself in ongoing training and workshops that sate her curiosity and interests. She enjoys a balanced and fulfilling life as the captain of her own ship.

She is actually living out her dream career.

If you had asked her in the days following the accident and retrenchment how she saw her future playing out, it's unlikely that she would have been able to foresee all the good that came from those unexpected events. But that's just it: it's tricky to see what might be on our horizons, especially when the potential positives are disguised as bad things that are happening to us.

Having the accident forced Wendy to stop and listen to her body, compelling her to focus on her physical recovery. Doing that gave her the clarity and the space to pursue her dream.

Would that have happened if she had not been obliged to zero in on her physical health? We will never know. But for Wendy, the link between her physical health and mental health was infinitely clear.

The bad things *are* actually bad, and we need to honour the feelings and losses that might come along with them. But it can also be true that difficult things mean the beginning of something new. The path forward is not always immediately clear, and it can take years before we feel we're ready to take those first tender steps, especially in the wake of a terrible loss. But that's okay—we don't have to have the answers or be able to see where our recovery from great loss might be leading us one day. Our only job is to process what has happened and ensure that we are looking after ourselves in the present moment. What comes next will unfold when we are ready.

Part of the self-care required after a plot twist is giving ourselves space to honour the spectrum of feelings that come bubbling up to the surface, some more persistent than others. It's imperative that we find healthy ways to work through our emotions: to feel, explore, unpack, wallow in, rinse and release them. Anything that involves expressing emotions outward—without, of course, harming others—is helpful. The last thing we want to do with our emotions is to bury them, avoid them or ignore them.

Feeling and expressing our emotions and being open to new paths are not mutually exclusive. As long as there is a little grain of hope inside, a sliver of positivity that keeps us moving forward, the new path will eventually become clear. Sometimes, a tiny little glimmer of hope is all we need to keep going.

When I chatted with the writer Emma Carey, she described a tiny pinprick of light—of hope—that shone through her blackout curtains during the darkest days of her life. That tiny piece of hope saw her clawing her way back from a devastating injury, an unspeakable shock and a psychological black hole.

Emma was fizzing with excitement as she embarked on the overseas adventure of a lifetime. Early on in her travels, she convinced her friend to go skydiving in the Swiss Alps. It was an opportunity to see the picturesque landscape from the sky—a once-in-a-lifetime experience.

In her book *The Girl Who Fell From the Sky*, Emma describes each moment of her two-minute fall from the helicopter door to the bone-shattering crash landing into the earth. She remembers every single detail from the fall to the landing, including the crushing weight of her skydiving instructor, who was unconscious and still strapped to her back, pinning her to the ground.

Emma sustained a spinal cord injury that meant she couldn't feel her legs from that moment onwards. What followed was a painful and slow recovery, a fragmented and warped perception of time and having to come to terms with a new reality that, at twenty years of age, had been the furthest thing from her mind.

It would be a terrifying prospect for anyone: to have the world in your palm in one moment, filled with possibility and adventure, followed by the literal crushing reality that your body can no longer do what it used to.

Although her life had come suddenly and violently to a halt in a very real way, Emma was able to find those tiny, micro moments of hope that helped her build up the strength to move forward. The way she did it was much like Wendy: by committing to her physical health and being reminded of the connection between mind and body.

Emma was inspired by the people she encountered in rehab who worked tirelessly through immense pain, sometimes for very little gain. She decided she was going to give as much to her recovery as they were, and formed a mindset that allowed her to focus on each part of her body that required it. Having the physical work to concentrate on gave Emma the determination to keep moving forward.

We don't need to fall out of a helicopter or acquire devastating injuries to remind ourselves of the mind and body connection. But it's remarkably easy to forget. When I'm feeling overwhelmed, anxious or stressed—when everything feels too hard and I'm ready to explode—I know the fastest way to decompress is to move my body.

But do you think I remember that in the moment? Absolutely not.

The Mind and Body Connection

Whenever I call my dad in a state of panic or anxiety, stress or overwhelm, the first thing he asks is how much exercise I'm doing. And like a brick to the head, I realise that the answer is *not enough*. It's incredible how easily that routine can slip, despite its being so imperative to improved mental health and better resilience for me. (And despite absolutely understanding the mind and body connection, as both a professional and a person who has experience with anxiety.)

Since having our third child, the busyness has never been more real. The moving parts and increased demands require a lot of time and energy. As someone who needs space and time alone to recharge, I've really thrown myself into the deep end here. But it's abundantly clear how vastly different my mood and ability to cope with the noise, mess and bedlam is when I've made time for exercise.

It can be as simple as walking my eldest to school and taking a brisk walk back on my own, with a podcast planted in my ears and no tiny people hanging from my appendages. That right there is a slice of heaven. Not only is it the alone time that's invaluable to me, it's the pounding of the pavement and moving my body to get the endorphins flowing.

When I'm at my best, I'm also adding in Pilates and yoga and dancing with the kids. It's just about moving my body, feeling the chemicals and the hormones shift and my anxious tension start to melt away. It doesn't disappear entirely, but just enough to help me reset and get a better grip on what's happening for me.

There is strong scientific evidence demonstrating the link between physical activity and better mental health. We know that exercise acts as a natural antidepressant. We have known about this research for years, but finding a way to make that link in our own lives can sometimes feel impossible. Especially when we're feeling distressed or at a loss. Even more so when we are in the throes of life's unexpected plot twists.

The link between mind and body is incredibly strong and can affect us in all kinds of ways. Our thoughts, feelings, beliefs and attitudes can have a positive or negative impact on our biological responses. It also works in reverse: what we eat, how much we move and even our posture can positively or negatively impact our mental health.

The benefits are clear: even just doing 30 minutes of exercise three to five times a week can significantly improve the symptoms of anxiety and depression. The trick is finding something you love and can do regularly—whether that's walking, running, an exercise class, dancing or swimming. I know that this can feel absolutely impossible at times, and the 'just do it' insistence from well-meaning people around us can feel like an affront. In those times, it's important to go gently on yourself and to take baby steps in the direction of movement. A walk to the letterbox for a start, or just making your way outside for some fresh air and sunlight. Sitting outside and rolling your ankles or stretching your arms overhead can increase oxygen flow through the body and can absolutely have a positive effect on your mood. Fractional changes to your routine and even just setting the intention and knowing that you *want* to move forward is worth celebrating. Recognising and celebrating even the tiniest of wins is important when the big moves feel so out of reach.

I know what you're thinking: it's just so easy to let the routine slip when things go south. Exercise and eating well are often the first things to fall off the priority list when life throws those enormous wrenches at you.

It's definitely what happens to me, and I know I'm not alone.

It's a common experience in bereavement, to be focused on the loss and trying to survive the tidal waves of emotions that come and go. It can be incredibly difficult to see what it is that your mind and body might actually need.

To the untrained eye, you still look exactly like the person you were before receiving the devastating news that threw your life into chaos. That in itself is one of the most difficult parts of any kind of sudden and unexpected loss—whether it's through bereavement, the ending of a relationship or the abrupt rupture of a dynamic you relied on. Having to reconcile the version of you that existed before with the newly wounded and never-the-same version now, while to the rest of the world you appear unchanged, is an absolute mind-bender. It's also incredibly isolating. It's strange and scary to suddenly feel completely alone, even while you're surrounded by the people you love. It's almost like an out-of-body experience when you no longer feel grounded or sure of your place in the world. Like a balloon that's just been let go of, hovering just out of reach of the people below.

The impact of grief and bereavement on our physical body is enormous. It can feel as though we're completely falling apart. From the endless fatigue and phantom body aches to extreme anxiety, headaches, tension and the very real symptoms of stress and burnout, it's a minefield. All of this hits, of course, when you have nothing left in the tank. No reserves to fight with, no resilience to bounce back with.

A friend described her experience with grief to me, and told me how she moved through the worst of it by leaning into her physicality. Diving into herself and doing the work from the inside out helped immensely to combat the complex layers of grief, trauma and anxiety that were battling it out inside her. As well as having a team of mental health professionals supporting her, she found that a focused approach to her physical being was imperative to her survival during this incredibly distressing time. She dedicated herself to doing breathwork and getting kinesiology and acupuncture to give her body the best chance of fighting through the darkness.

What will work for one person may not even touch the sides for someone else. In fact, what worked last time we fell apart may not have the same power for us the next time, so trying new things and experimenting with strategies is important with each loss.

When we're faced with the biggest challenges in our lives, focusing on the things that we can control can help to soften the fear and unrest that comes with the things we can't. By starting with our physical health—ensuring we are keeping our engines running with good food, plenty of water and rest, movement, meditation, breathwork, mindfulness and whatever else works—we are filling our cups from within, giving ourselves the gift of self-care.

It's just so important to keep on moving. This doesn't have to mean pounding the pavement for hours at a time or forcing ourselves into classes or activities that we wouldn't ordinarily do. (Although they can be helpful, of course.) Sometimes it's more about that connection to our bodies—learning to listen and work out what they need is a practice in itself.

When we're in the middle of a crisis and are heightened emotionally, we can find ourselves spiralling into stress and overwhelm. One of my clients felt this keenly. Lisa had just retired from a high-level finance career that had been very demanding of her time and mental space. She and her husband were looking forward to finally being able to spend time travelling Australia together: joining the great tradition of grey nomads journeying up to the Top End.

Lisa and I giggled at the idea of her trading in her high-flying corporate life and chic designer gear for a pair of cargo pants and an enamel mug for those end-of-day drinks. For Lisa and David, her husband of more than 40 years, that dream was on the precipice of becoming a reality. After spending their entire working lives in the rat race, they were ready to slow right down and savour their time together.

Devastatingly, those plans never came to fruition. David passed away suddenly in his sleep one night. Lisa's entire world came to a standstill. Her future, her plans for the next chapter of her life, all disappeared overnight.

As Lisa and her family scrambled to make sense of this loss and began the difficult task of trying to piece together a new future without David, the family was struck by another devastating blow. Just a few short months after losing David, their youngest daughter was involved in a car accident. After some time in hospital, tragically, she lost her life.

For Lisa, the grief was, of course, immense. She described feeling stunned by her body's response to her losses. The physical pain and the emotional distress were all-consuming. Every part of her body ached. It throbbed in agony.

When we met, Lisa described her experience with bewilderment, saying 'Jana, this is the level of stress I felt in my body during the highest-stress times at work—my body remembers this.' Although the consecutive, devastating losses were entirely different to what she'd experienced on the trading floor, Lisa's experience of the stress response made complete sense.

The Mind and Body Connection

As a highly successful woman working in a very high-pressure role, Lisa was accustomed to her body being flooded with cortisol and bracing itself in fight, flight or freeze. The way she managed that at work was to throw her type A, rational and logical brain at the issues and solve them in an organised and consistent way. She'd break down each hurdle as it appeared in front of her, using reason and a wealth of experience.

Grief and bereavement don't exactly work like that, though. There's no rationalising your way out of it. Lisa was suffering through unimaginable pain and sadness, and the signals that her body was sending her were familiar on a cellular level. She recognised that resurfacing stress, burnout and overwhelm as byproducts of her grief. As an active person, Lisa already had a regular exercise habit, so moving her body wasn't a problem. What she found was that she was in a constant battle with her brain, which wanted to leap into action to combat and resolve those devastating losses. The pain was profound and her brain wanted to rescue her, because it knew just what to do with those signals of overwhelm: organise, plan, attack.

But because there was no action for her to take, no left-brain resolution to these terrible tragedies, Lisa found herself burning out at a much faster rate. She couldn't make decisions and every task from the menial to the major was leaving her wheels spinning.

The way out of this for Lisa was to mindfully do nothing. She had to make this an intentional choice. To quieten her mind, to slow the overwhelm, she practised—for the first time in her over-achieving life—sitting in the discomfort of the noise in her mind and choosing to do nothing. For Lisa, just like so many of us, resisting the urge to solve and resolve, to scramble for answers and organise her way out of things, was incredibly difficult.

If you have a busy mind, learning to disengage and connect with your body in stillness can feel counterintuitive. The idea that to neutralise the effects of overwhelm you might need to switch off and do nothing, when all of your success and achievements and habits in life revolve around the *doing*, is the ultimate headspin.

However, actually slowing down is another way to propel ourselves into forward motion, just in a less obvious way. Activity and movement isn't always going to be the answer. For some, the answer will be stillness. Dedicating a window of time to actively choosing to do nothing gives your brain a chance to decompress, to switch off from the natural instinct to solve a problem that is unsolvable.

Engaging in this process is about reconnecting with our bodies in a calm and safe space, tuning in to the things that we might need and stopping the relentless scramble that is going on in our minds and bodies when we're in crisis mode. Lisa did this by blocking out half an hour each day to lie on the floor of her lounge room and do nothing. She described the experience as excruciating to begin with. She had to find new ways to drown out the noise in her head. She tried podcasts and music in the background, and reported that she actually had to visualise herself putting a pen and paper down on the desk to symbolise an imposed period of non-work. This helped encourage her mind to stop listing tasks and thinking through her responsibilities, and instead sink in to stillness and rest.

The benefits of being in a near-meditative state are endless. Having a designated time to switch off and be still calms the nervous system, which is so often going haywire when we're in crisis. The distress of loss or unexpected change can wreak havoc on our adrenals, our nervous system and, of course, our mental health. All of that internal activity drains us of our energy and stamina, and our ability to concentrate and make effective decisions. This, in turn, leaves us feeling depleted and tapped out. When that happens, there's nothing left—no gas in the tank to keep the machine going. Our feelings feel bigger, they're harder to manage and we can lose hope and sight of the bigger picture.

Meditation in its traditional form doesn't work for everyone. But a meditative state can be found while walking outside, while practising yoga, during time on the couch, in the garden or at the beach. The key to finding that state is to give yourself the space and permission to just *be*.

We are all hyperaware of the busyness of this current way of life. We are constantly squeezing whatever we can into tiny windows of time. We're packing our lives full of commitments and responsibilities, then berating ourselves when we don't make time for our friends, our loved ones or ourselves, because we're too busy or burnt out and can't possibly fit another thing in.

Broadcaster, author and media personality Yumi Stynes shared the same sentiments in our conversation for *The Curious Life*. She argued that, in fact, we all *love* to be busy and that it's tied to feeling important. For Yumi, finding the balance is quite simple: it's about getting an endorphin hit every day through running and vigorous exercise, sometimes twice if she can, and taking a pause—a moment to inhale instead of cramming every minute full of activities and busyness. That pause can involve meditation. It can also be getting into a flow state in the kitchen, where she intentionally finds a moment to inhabit her physical self and the space she is occupying and listens to what her body is trying to tell her.

We can all do that in our own way: stripping back the layers of needs and wants and making time—just the tiniest bit each day—to connect with ourselves at our core. It's easy to forget that we are living, breathing organisms that need water and sunlight and fresh air. Connecting with our bodies, understanding them, feeding them and nourishing them through movement and stillness is one of the greatest gifts we can give ourselves. It pays dividends via the energy and motivation that is restored when we listen to what our bodies need.

When we're in the practice of doing this, it's much easier to rely on and prioritise when life pulls a fast one on us. It's like having a secret weapon in our back pockets.

THINGS TO CONSIDER

➤ *Our bodies and our minds are so closely connected that it's often a chicken-or-egg problem. When you're feeling overwhelmed, stressed, anxious or emotional, consider whether this could be because you haven't been moving your body. Or is it a response to your loss? It may be both, which means moving will make a difference.*

➤ *Ask yourself: Can I combat some of this pain I'm experiencing by doing something different with my body?*

➤ *Experiment with a new form of movement this week—something high intensity, or a slow morning stroll around the block, a yoga class or a social sport. Take advantage of those feel-good endorphins post-exercise. If this sounds like too much, then reel it back in and try taking some of those baby steps instead. Intention is the very first step.*

7

Finding What Works

When life has taken a sharp turn and we find ourselves facing a different future than the one we had first imagined, finding those little glimmers of hope can be like looking for a needle in a haystack. But I'm here to tell you: even if it feels like it's impossible now, you *will* find your way back to a hopeful life again.

In the early days, regaining forward motion can be the hardest part. Building up the drive to keep going can feel like an insurmountable task. But the singular effort of putting one foot in front of the other plays a big role in moving through the hardest parts.

So, where do we get the energy to take that next step? Through hope. Hope is the currency of forward motion. It's to be found in the golden dreams that we cling to, that keep us warm at night, that fill our hearts with courage. Find hope and it can mean that, just maybe, we might be ready to take the first step. Just the tiniest bit of hope can help us start building a pathway towards our next destination.

For each of us, that path will look different.

After my boyfriend jetted off overseas without me, I entered a long period of singledom. Eight years, in fact. During this time the people I loved spoke reassuring words but they could not fill the void within me. Their gentle encouragement about my potential future fell on deaf ears. Every time someone close to me said, 'You just have to be patient! Less picky! It will happen when you least expect it!' I would nod and smile and thank them for their sage advice, but inside I was brewing a fervent inner storm of insecurity and uncertainty. What made those happily coupled-up friends of mine so sure that it would happen for me, too? What did my family know about where my life would end up? My inner turmoil grew as the years whizzed by, and the rejections and hangovers became part of my *Sex and the City* life.

In the eight years that I was single and going through the motions on Tinder 1.0, I met some great guys and some terrible ones. I gave dating a red-hot go. I had wild nights out with friends, met random guys in bars (do people do that anymore?) and held on to the hope that I would meet 'the one' and live out the fantasy life of a fulfilling relationship and a houseful of kids.

All of my friends were in long-term or serious relationships that were, in quick succession, leading to engagements, hens' parties and weddings. My own happy ending felt further and further away with each celebration I attended.

Meanwhile, my personal revolving door of short-term, unrequited or utterly disappointing connections was eating away at my confidence that I would, as everyone assured me, find the right man—the perfect partner for me.

One particular birthday I was driving home from the lovely dinner I had just spent with my dad and brother celebrating little old single me, and I broke down into tears at the steering wheel. I remember saying to my dad, 'What if it never happens for me? What if I'm alone forever?' It was the first time I had spoken those words out loud. In that moment, I truly felt that fear and sadness with more honesty and vulnerability than I had ever allowed myself to admit.

It felt completely unfair that I had been through all of this turmoil and still hadn't quite found my way back upright.

My friends all seemed to have it figured out. Were they that much more attractive as a future prospect than I was? It felt like everywhere I turned, there was another announcement or celebration to swallow, stampeding down my Facebook feed and reminding me over and over again that my story was not that.

It's a difficult thing to reconcile when you're in the eye of the experience. As a young woman in her twenties with enormous losses to process, perhaps I wasn't ready in that moment to leap into the next chapter of my life. I had some learning and some growing to do. But, boy, did it raise the anxiety levels and throw me deep into that completely unhelpful comparison trap where I measured my own life and successes against those of my peers.

Journalist and author Nell Frizzell writes about the 'panic years': those anxiety-riddled years where women, in particular, feel a biological, psychological and societal pressure and expectation to springboard into the next phase of our adult lives. Partners, children, mortgages, careers: when they're not all exactly where we think they *should* be compared to our peers and the population at large, we can spiral into panic and distress at the lack of forward motion. I experienced those panic years intensely; though, if I'm honest, I concealed it pretty well with my void-filling partying, busy schedule and endless nights out. I was always having fun, but the undercurrent of anxiety was there.

Shortly after meeting my current partner Chris, when he was still just an exciting new connection I had made and was hopeful about (as I had been with other men so many times before), I went to see a psychic medium who a colleague had recommended. It wasn't my first time dipping into the spiritual realm: I had been to see a psychic not long after Mum died and had an incredibly moving and validating experience. I was excited to see this psychic as I knew that she had brought a lot of clarity and reassurance to my colleague through a tumultuous time in her personal life.

Elizabeth Muir was about to change my entire outlook on life and the universe around me.

Meeting with Liz for the first time, I was buzzing with nervous energy and hoping to hear one way or another what was in store for me in the coming year. Before I had even fully sat down in the chair, she told me something about my aunty that only the immediate family would have known at the time. She then completely knocked my socks off when she said, 'I know this because your mum is telling me.'

Boom. Mind blown. I had not provided my full name and there was no way she could have tricked her way to any of the information that flowed from her so effortlessly: things that no one could have known. She described my new connection with Chris in minute detail and revealed things about our budding relationship that were so specific that I had no choice but to believe. Each new piece of information about me, my new love interest and my life in general was like a little bubble of assurance, bursting into the river of my consciousness. That one session provided me with so much clarity and hope that I left the appointment fizzing with renewed energy and excitement about what the future would bring.

Having that reassurance, even if I wasn't entirely sure if it was magic or reality, freed me from the anxiety that had wound its way around my heart and loosened the vice grip it had on my panicked hopes for the future.

It also meant that I was able to give things up to the universe. I wasn't entirely sure what I thought or believed in a spiritual sense, but Liz had shown me things that made me realise I didn't need to have all the answers to give myself over to the experience. Letting go of my attachment to the outcome of my life and, in effect, trusting that things would unfold the way they were supposed to enabled me to breathe new life into my existence. I felt a freedom within myself that I hadn't felt in years.

That freedom and release meant that things started to click into place very quickly after that. The pavement had cracked open, and the flowers were pushing up through the gaps. I honestly felt an enormous shift and renewed belief that everything was as it should be. Up until that point, I realised that I was tensed in a defensive position, unconsciously bracing for the next bad thing to happen. Expecting the worst, even in the good times. Opening myself up to the notion of a power greater than myself, whatever it was, call it the universe, spirituality, manifestation, enveloped me in a sense of peace and smudged out the isolation that had followed me after all of those upheavals. I felt supported and was no longer hustling on my own.

Finding a sense of purpose and belief will look different for each of us, but when we get to that place of psychological calm and purposeful action, that is what keeps us in the present. It's a mindful acknowledgement of living in the now, rather than reaching for the past or future. This is where true change begins. And I truly felt the transformation taking place within me.

For some of my clients at the Coroners Court, mindful acceptance of their life's circumstances meant that they were leaning into or away from their own religious or spiritual beliefs. I remember talking about this with one of my clients, Mark, following the unimaginable loss of his son to suicide. A parent never, ever recovers from this. This man, broken and forever changed in every way possible, would come to see me every week after losing his only son. For weeks and weeks, he would go over every detail of his son's life in the lead-up to his death. He turned over every stone in his mind to try to make sense of this senseless loss. This was his way of processing the relentless pain that he was enduring, every moment of every day. He never failed to attend an appointment, bursting into the office with purpose and always punctual. In each session he was going down the same rabbit holes, searching for meaning and understanding about how his son could possibly have done this. He was hoping that in considering every possibility, he would somehow come to the answer that he was so desperately searching for.

One day, the conversation turned to his beliefs about what happens after we die. Without a moment's hesitation, almost as if this was the least important consideration, he said that this part didn't bother him at all. He knew for certain where his son was, and that he would see him again. He was a deeply religious man, and his conviction came from his lifetime of faith. This meant that he had no concerns or questions at all about what happened to his son *after* his death. He was completely at peace within his belief that his son was in a beautiful place, and that they would be reunited again when it was his time to pass.

He moved the conversation on. The *after* wasn't what was distressing him; it was the *now* that was causing him to suffer. He knew where his son's spirit had gone, but he desperately wanted to understand how he had gotten there.

This was in stark contrast to other clients'—and indeed my own—questions about life and death, and whether or not there is an afterlife. This topic was a big part of the processing for so many non-religious and non-spiritual people that I worked with. The distress and anxiety around where their loved ones had gone compounded the loss and grief for so many.

I envied Mark and his implicit belief in the next phase of the soul's journey. It simplified his grief and stripped back the many layers of distress and confusion that weigh so heavily on many of us following a loss. That clarity was his panacea. Mark found what worked for him—unconditional belief in his religion and its teachings. Although it didn't completely absolve him of pain, it gave him a support system to lean into during the most painful times.

This absolute belief in a higher power is shared by Sara, a beautiful friend of mine who was raging through her panic years, as I was, when we first met in Bali many years ago.

I was shocked and devastated to learn recently that Sara had been diagnosed with a terminal brain cancer. She had already outlived her doctors' expectations, but the prospects were grim. Sara is a vibrant and bright young woman, filled with endless possibilities and potential, whose life has taken the most drastic of turns. Just a few years younger than me, she has been robbed of the gift of a promising future. Life does not throw any bigger curveballs than this.

Hearing Sara's news gave me yet another grave reality check about the brevity of life and just how quickly things can change.

When we reconnected by phone, I was astonished to discover that Sara's incredible warmth and light had not dimmed one iota. We talked at length about the chain of events that led to where she was now, how she coped with the devastating blows that drastically changed the course of her life and how she managed to maintain her buoyancy and positive outlook throughout.

The answer surprised me. She had returned to her Catholic roots, through an unplanned interaction with a priest who ignited within her a deep connection to her faith.

If I were in Sara's shoes I imagine I would be frightened out of my mind: an anxious, fretting mess. Yet Sara has found peace. She has freed herself from apprehension and fear and is truly living joyfully and in the moment. She isn't worrying about the future or the past; she is living for today without any expectations about tomorrow.

This is something I find incredibly inspiring, as that kind of mindful living is something I have found very difficult in the tougher moments of my life. However, this is absolutely not about buying into organised religion. It's not something I personally subscribe to in the slightest. But it *is* about finding what works for you.

Religion or spirituality won't work for everyone. In my professional world I have seen just as many clients turn away from their faith following loved ones' sudden and tragic deaths as towards it. In some cases people felt abandoned and betrayed at the highest level. They could not fathom how their god could be so cruel as to have taken away their precious person under such circumstances, leaving them to endure such relentless suffering. Their conclusion was that there could not possibly be a god who could cause so much pain. Understandably, they walked away from their beliefs.

Others found themselves questioning their faith. Curious about new ways of thinking, they were propelled into searching for meaning via other avenues. Those people understood what no longer worked for them.

Finding that thing we can run towards is part of the way we continue moving forward, even when terrible things have happened.

Acclaimed psychiatrist Phil Stutz talks about the notion of living in forward motion. He and his colleague, psychotherapist

Barry Michels, theorised that one of the greatest challenges that so many of us face is our completely human response to pain. To protect ourselves from any level of pain—be that rejection, grief, fear of failure or any of the other myriad causes—we run in the other direction. We evade it, procrastinate, avoid taking risks; we will do anything to spare ourselves the anguish that the perceived pain may bring us. But Stutz and Michels believe that when we run *towards* our pain we build up our tolerance to those sometimes-unbearable feelings. And that is when we are living in forward motion.

So how do we run towards the pain, to build up that tolerance to grief and rejection and fear? We have to sit in that stickiness of pain and discomfort and give ourselves permission to be all the things that we might be in those circumstances.

In my case, during that blindside breakup, I should have faced the big feelings head-on and been more honest about what it all meant. Looking back now, I wish that I'd had the courage to actually cut the whole thing off at the knees years before I finally did. It would have saved a lot of emotional turmoil and anguish. Instead of running towards the pain, I ran away from it in the form of denial and hope for a future that wouldn't have served me (or him). I held on to a crumbling idea of what it had once been, out of fear of what it really meant to be on my own. Instead of moving through the layers of pain, I shelved them and stayed stuck, treading water in a pond I had outgrown.

For Mark and Sara, it's their unconditional belief in their faith that propels them forward. For me, it was opening my eyes to new ideas and believing that there is a higher power, the universe or fate, that means we all eventually land on the path we are meant to. It's not a catch-all enduring belief, however. There are frequently times when I'll need a top-up of that clarity or some serious work on my self-talk and outlook to bring me out of worry or anxiety, and back into a mindful place. But leaning into those experiences helped propel me forward in the knowledge that there was something bigger than me, than my pain and my angst, that meant all of it would be worth it one day.

For you, it might be something completely different. But whatever it is, it's the notion of moving forward, not becoming stuck in anguish or falling victim to circumstances. We have to keep believing that we deserve good things and that there is hope on the other side of pain. We have to keep moving.

THINGS TO CONSIDER

- *Talk to people, listen to podcasts, read books, try new things and you'll find that not only have countless others experienced what you are going through right at this very minute, countless more will, too. What did they do to process their pain? What worked for them?*

➜ *Take a leaf out of my book and connect with a psychic. Break out of your comfort zone, even if it feels a bit silly at first.*

➜ *Ask yourself: Can I channel my energy into the things that work for me, and drown out others' noise?*

➜ *What works for you this time might look different next time. Once again, go gently. Cut yourself a break if you're finding yourself up against an imaginary wall instead of moving forward with intention.*

➜ *Listen to what your body is telling you and how it is responding to the things you are doing. Your gut will tell you if you're on the right track. And once you've found that thing—run towards it.*

8

The Language of Loss

When we are in crisis mode or our world has imploded, it's important to have the language to make sense of what is happening to us. If we haven't been through sudden loss or change before, it can be hard to identify what is happening in our internal landscape. Without being able to articulate how we're feeling it can all just feel like a tangled mess of distress.

When I was going through my sudden plot twists, I knew that I was in pain. I knew I felt awfully sad, but I didn't quite know the extent of what I was going through or how it might continue to affect me in the years to come. The overarching themes of my feelings were unmissable, but I didn't actually know where to start when it came to peeling back the layers and integrating the losses in any way.

The ability to reflect on our experience isn't something that is automatic for everyone. The more we go through, the more adept we can become at explaining and understanding how it might affect us. These are important skills that don't just magically appear overnight.

As a therapist, I've learned a lot of language through my work—ways of understanding emotion and behaviour and reflecting observations back to people. I've also learned a lot through my own life experiences, both the good and the bad. I have always been a ponderer: someone who enjoys examining and sharing my innermost thoughts with the people I feel close to. It helps me to do that work verbally, unpacking my responses and reactions and working out where they have come from, or why I feel the way I do.

When I'm going through something, it's important for me to untangle that mess of feelings and the responses I might have to a situation. This process helps me to understand what's going on for me, and to articulate it to others. It also helps me feel more in control of my situation, and helps me feel heard when I can then share it with others.

For example, if I've had a big reaction to something that's happening at home, instead of just blowing up or stewing on it (okay, maybe *after* I've done those things) I untangle and analyse it. I can't just let it go and move on; my brain will be trying to resolve it or make sense of it, even in the background.

Then suddenly I'll think, 'Ohhh, I must have been reacting like that because I'm overwhelmed and run-down, and I was already feeling triggered/stressed/anxious about that other thing that's unresolved/unfinished/undetected.'

Putting the pieces together gives me an explanation for my feelings or behaviour and provides relief that feels like an 'Aha' moment. The process helps me understand how I operate when I'm in crisis mode or when something unexpected happens. Knowing how my brain works and how I make sense of things helps me move through difficult situations. It's also about identifying my trigger points: knowing where I've come from, what has happened and why it makes me feel a certain way.

However, sitting in difficult feelings and processing them in this way doesn't come naturally to everyone. And it's never a straightforward, overnight process for me, either. You might find it's actually an extremely uncomfortable place for you to be. That may be because of past experiences, the way you were raised, family dynamics or the culture you grew up with. Or it might be that you simply don't have the language to express what is going on for you, or the right set of ears to receive it.

When you're feeling uncomfortable with your emotions or unclear about what is bubbling away beneath the surface, the best thing for future you is to throw yourself into the ring. Confront those feelings head-on. Sometimes saying it all out loud can be confronting. Instead, you could start with journalling, free writing all that mess of emotion in whatever capacity it comes to you: dot points, sentences, angry scrawl. Just writing out your feelings can help uncover what is really going on underneath. Setting a time to do this each day, every few days or even once a week is a good habit to get into. It alerts your brain to the fact that this is important and is the set time when you are going to get uncomfortable. An assigned moment of reflection and exploration.

Finding the words to identify, explain and understand your feelings is one thing; having opportunities to share them is another. Both are important pieces of recovery from whatever it is that has thrown you off kilter or marked the end of a chapter.

Sometimes you might need to have a look at the way you share your thoughts and feelings with others. Begin the conversation with sentences that start with 'I feel like . . .' or 'When this happens, it makes me feel . . .' This also gets you into the habit of pausing and reflecting on what it is that you're actually feeling, instead of responding with a kneejerk reaction or response that isn't congruent with your emotions. By using these 'I' statements, we intentionally pull the focus back onto ourselves, rather than deflecting from the real feelings we might be experiencing. It's always easier to avoid those big feelings, rather than confront them. Using 'I feel' at the start of the sentence helps us to zero in on what we are really responding to, instead of being distracted by the noise around us.

When your language or communication style don't align with the person you're trying to get vulnerable with, this can create a missed opportunity for exploration and growth. If you leave a conversation feeling drained when the intention was to seek support for yourself, that might be a sign that you are misaligned in that moment. Sometimes the people closest to us are not best equipped to handle the bigger conversations we might be needing to have. Support might come in the surprising form of a work colleague or newer friend, instead of the people who have known you the longest. It can be difficult to hear what someone might really be saying when we are deeply imbedded in each other's lives. You will know if that person is the right fit for the kind of exploration you find yourself moving towards. You will feel heard, seen and understood. If you leave the conversation feeling confused, questioned or misunderstood, then perhaps they just weren't the right person at the right time.

I've been thinking a lot lately about the impact of relationships ending. There are entire industries that have been created to monetise heartbreak. Films, books, music, cards and gifts that are marketed to those of us going through a breakup. Even ice cream has been branded as the breakup food of choice.

When someone chooses to end a relationship, while it can be sad and difficult, it can also be the beginning of something new: a different chapter they were open to exploring, even if it's painful. For the dumpee, however, it can feel very much like the ending: an enormous chasm that rips through every part of the life they once knew, the tectonic plates of their internal landscape torn wide open.

Okay, it's not always as dramatic as that; but for some, the ending of a relationship can feel as severe and painful as a death.

Recently a friend of mine went through a sudden and inexplicable breakup. Jamie and her partner had been married for eight years but together much longer than that. The loss sent her spiralling into a very dark place where she was unable to see the light at all. There were complex layers to process. Her distress was immense. The reconfiguring of their family added to the many wounds she was suffering—there were changing dynamics and shifting goal posts as she tried to navigate co-parenting with her ex. Each time the arrangements had to change it would throw her.

Compounding all of this was Jamie's constant worry about the impact the breakup was having on her children. She was concerned about the long-term effect the separation would have on her kids, and how her former partner was seemingly able to disconnect from this. The worry took a significant toll on her mental health.

Jamie and her ex had very different communication styles and ways of grieving. The way he was moving through this enormous loss felt jarring to my friend, and the distinction between them pushed her deeper into the abyss. It was not only the breakdown of the marriage that caused her great pain, but also the sudden severing of the connection between them. She had felt that the relationship was on reasonably solid ground prior to this. In the space of a single conversation, she had gone from a busy working mum with a predictable and stable home life, to navigating this new world of anguish and despair, worry and concern—without her best friend and partner in life by her side. She'd lost her partner, her family unit, her identity and her future.

Suddenly she couldn't recognise her former partner anymore. Jamie was shocked by his decisions and his certainty about the relationship being over. Her confidant, the person she had known and loved for well over a decade, was gone. In his place was a painful reminder of everything she had lost. He became a place for her to direct her anger and confusion, but no longer a safe person for her to share her pain or feelings with.

Jamie went through every emotion on the spectrum: distress, grief, anger, disbelief, outrage, fury, darkness, loneliness, desperation, confusion, vulnerability, rawness, pain. Nothing made sense to her. Her entire world had been blown up; she scrambled every day to pick up the fragments that had been blasted all over the memories of her old life.

To pour a mountain of salt on this incredibly fresh wound, her former partner appeared to be living his best life after the separation. He became lighter, unburdened, relishing in the new arrangements. His ending of the relationship had given him the gift of time to explore his identity, try new things and shake himself free of his old life. Seeing him flourish and thrive in his independence was devastating to Jamie. The pain of this began to bleed into her reflections of their time together, causing her to question everything and wonder whether any of it had, in fact, been real. Everything was up for evaluation: who he was, who she was, who they were as a couple.

Jamie's own life ground to a relative halt. She couldn't work, avoided friends and was barely functioning.

When we go through something as devastating as the breakup of a family, it can put a match to old embers of pain and loss, reigniting the flame and bringing the visceral memories to the surface.

In my friend's case, her old traumas and grief resurfaced, compounding the anguish she was experiencing through the breakdown of her marriage. She didn't have the language to express the breadth of her pain and fears, and she was avoiding sharing this in detail with others.

Like many of us, Jamie had experienced many losses in her life but she had never truly worked through them. By the time her marriage ended she had a significant amount of cumulative grief that she had not addressed. The relationship ending unblocked the dam and the waters of distress came flooding into her system. This overwhelmed her completely and she didn't know how to even begin to pick herself up and keep moving.

To be fair, having to regroup after a family separation can be incredibly difficult for anyone. For my friend, however, it was even more gruelling as she was already weighed down by her snowballing, unresolved, unexplored experiences.

When she was ready and with quite a bit of prompting, she began seeing a therapist to begin the inner work she had been avoiding.

Avoidance is a very common response to the big events in our lives. When we are consumed with anxiety, fear, overwhelm or heartache, avoidance is a natural response. Instead of running towards the discomfort, as Phil Stutz recommends, we automatically close in on ourselves and stay well within our comfort zone. That sounds a whole lot cushier than it actually is. During periods of grief or loss, staying within our comfort zone can actually mean staying within the sadness and pain.

Facing the pain head-on and unpacking the deeper feelings can feel impossible. Instead, we tend to avoid our feelings, and the activities or interactions that remind us of these unresolved issues, thereby doing nothing about them.

When our path has become unclear and our feelings have gone haywire, there are other unsung emotions underneath the obvious ones. We're usually aware of the loudest feelings, such as anger, sadness and grief. But beneath those are often less obvious emotions such as abandonment, insecurity or a scary little feeling called vulnerability. When we feel vulnerable we feel exposed, unprotected and raw. Acknowledging and sinking into that vulnerability can feel like an enormous risk to take—deep, dark waters to dive into. It's incredible the lengths our brain will go to so we can avoid feeling vulnerable, especially if we haven't dipped into it before. We buck ourselves up, build up impenetrable walls, put on our masks and avoid it at all costs. This can look like denial, defensiveness, deflection. It's so common that we often do it without even realising.

But despite it *feeling* incredibly scary and counterintuitive, pushing through those feelings of discomfort and pain and allowing ourselves to acknowledge that vulnerability—and, even better, to share it—is actually incredibly brave.

Vulnerability is what sits underneath the anxiety when you feel as though everything is spinning out of your control. In Jamie's case, she felt as though her entire life had spun away from her, totally out of grasp.

There were three things that made her struggle so much deeper and prevented her from finding her way out of it easily. (All three, by the way, were totally, utterly understandable. What she was going through was inexplicably difficult.)

First, she just didn't have the language, the psychological shorthand, to examine her experience. She also didn't really want to. She was resisting talking with friends about what had happened; she didn't want to go to therapy at first (which is a great place to land when you don't want to talk with family or friends about it), and took the burden on alone, entirely to her own detriment. It ate her up, burned her out and wore her down.

Second, she avoided her real feelings about it. She hovered somewhere near the surface of those terribly murky waters, auto-piloting through the logistics and the anger and sadness, but not wanting to get into the weeds and confront the pain and past traumas.

Third, she was trying desperately to control the uncontrol-lable. This is a natural instinct in all of us: when the shit hits the fan, we spiral because we cannot control so much of what is happening to us. In this case, Jamie fought against the inevita-ble, blazed through her limited energy reserves and didn't have much left for anything else. She spent her time wrestling with the details of the separation and the custody arrangements, fighting tooth and nail over every detail that arose. She didn't acquiesce about anything, even when she would actually have benefited from whatever arrangement she was fighting on principle.

She swam upstream, until she could not swim anymore.

When she finally relented, and began to let go of some of the issues that were well and truly out of her control—such as her partner's decision about the relationship, and parts of the legal and co-parenting agreements—she began to feel some of the anxiety ease. This made way for her vulnerability to speak.

From there, she started to feel ready to begin her journey of self-discovery. She embarked on her first experience of therapy. She was surprised how much there was to work through. Part of her resistance to therapy was thinking she knew what was going on for her, and what on earth could anyone else do about it? It wasn't going to change the outcome, it wasn't going to restore her family unit, so what was the point?

I completely understood what she meant.

I've talked of this before, in my own stubborn refusal to address my own grief after losing my mum. I thought I knew it all! I knew why I was in pain; it was glaringly obvious. I had lost my mum—no conversation about it could make that better or bring her back. So, what was the point?

Now, of course, I know exactly what the point was. Talking with a professional wouldn't make my pain so brilliantly healed that I would bounce back into life as if nothing had ever happened. Therapy was about discovering all the hidden traumas and losses—primary and secondary—and learning the language to identify which parts of me were struggling the most so I could understand myself on a deeper level. Therapy gave me the tools to understand myself and how I relate to the world. It taught me how to be vulnerable and share my experiences in a meaningful way.

And that's just the tip of the iceberg, really.

All of us have underlying issues that influence how we respond to challenges. When something big and unexpected happens, we're robbed of the luxury of rational thinking and comprehensive analysis of our emotions. That comes later.

To get there, we need to be open to understanding the breadth of human emotion and finding our own language to express it.

Discovering other ways of looking at our losses can also shed light on what else might be happening for us. There is always something to be learned from each new experience—even the painful ones. Knowing that there are different ways to express and articulate what we're going through can help us to connect with what's really going on underneath the surface. This is one of the ways that we integrate and consolidate negative experiences once we're through the immediate aftermath.

Don't be afraid to dig right down and discover what's beneath the bigger and more palpable emotions you're feeling. It's not always as obvious as you think.

THINGS TO CONSIDER

➤ *New language isn't going to just find its way to you. You have to actively seek it out in conversation with others, in therapy or through other mediums that encourage you to learn and grow.*

➤ *Ask yourself: What part of my loss am I interested to learn more about?*

➤ *Try reading books by new-to-you authors, find experts you connect with and listen to inspiring or engaging speakers on mental health, grief, wellness and wellbeing.*

➤ *Practise opening up to your own experience through journalling, letter writing or recording voice notes to yourself.*

➤ *Try having more meaningful conversations with the people you feel close to. Share some of what your experience has been like—even if what you went through feels like a long way in the past.*

9

Relationshifts

There is a lot of chat in this book about life's big plot twists: the deaths of people we love, the ending of romantic relationships. Those are enormous losses, and important periods of growth can flower from them—there's no doubt about it.

But in our vast and complex lifetimes there are many other shifts and ruptures that can cause a huge amount of pain. These can equally prompt us to reflect and reconsider our path, our position or our perspective on life. Sometimes these more nuanced changes can have a ripple effect on our mental health and well-being. Many of our relationships will look and feel different after a plot twist as we re-evaluate our boundaries and priorities.

Every relationship we have with the people in our lives, from our friends and family members to our colleagues and collaborators, fulfils a different part of us and provides us with nourishment in distinctive ways. The connections we have with our peers and our friends, our lifelong and new friendships, meet a range of different needs we have as human beings.

When those relationships end or the dynamics shift in a big way it can be just as earth-shattering and difficult to move through as when a romantic relationship ends. The loss we feel when we lose a friendship is one of those deep losses that isn't commonly talked about. It can feel almost shameful when a connection ends outside of our control.

As a woman I understand that friendship with other women is essential to my being. Yet it's so easy to forget just how important these connections are when I'm caught up in the busyness of life. I've been particularly guilty of that in recent years. Now, coming out the other side of it, I'm filled with yearning and regret for the time I haven't spent with my closest friends.

The pandemic damaged many of our connections, mine included. During those three years we were in and out of lockdown we spent so much time sequestered away in our homes, alone or with families, gradually losing the skills of socialisation. Before the pandemic I would have considered myself a highly engaged friend. I had a big network of school friends, uni friends from both undergraduate and postgraduate study, and previous and current work friends. My roster was long but the connections were also incredibly real and deep. My calendar was filled with girls' nights, dinners, lunches, wine time, park and beach hangs, birthdays, walks, cafe visits, weekends away—even with young kids, we all made our friendships a priority. Time with my friends was non-negotiable and a big part of my identity. Friends were a crucial part of my support system and the way that I nourished my soul.

Then, as a Melbourne resident, I found myself in the most locked-down city in the world (hello, plot twist). And I didn't hate it. The pace of life slowed right down—ground to a halt, in fact. There was no pressure to keep up with a runaway train of invitations and social expectations. The fear of missing out was gradually replaced by the joy of missing out.

That was undoubtedly the biggest plot twist for many millions of us through Covid. As an outgoing introvert, I found the extra time at home actually suited me. I could also write reams and reams of pages about the anxiety and fear of daily life at that time, of course; I remember hours spent glued to the television for the latest updates and statistics about the increasing risks and danger of this mysterious and deadly virus.

The fear of the virus itself was one thing; the impact of the climate of anxiety and alarm from a social perspective was quite another. While the intention was to keep our communities safe and protect our most vulnerable (objectives I was absolutely in support of), the unintentional side-effect was that we become paranoid and fearful of others. We began to see other people—the unmasked, the unvaccinated, those we walked by in our authorised allotment of exercise time within five kilometres of our homes—as risks to our safety, just because we were breathing in shared air as we passed them anonymously in the park.

In the first year of lockdown, we all took to Zoom with the enthusiasm of the Boxing Day sales. We Zoomed birthdays, dinners and trivia nights with friends. We had virtual drinks and joined House Party. There was a thrill in the unknown and a bolstered sense of global community, knowing that most of the world was going through the same experiences we were. We were all living through a universal plot twist, unprecedented by anything like it in living memory. I felt incredibly blessed to be journeying through this scary time in the safety of a very privileged world with a strong medical system and the luxury of space, electricity, wi-fi and clean water.

However, the novelty began to wear off pretty quickly. Zoom trivia and virtual catch-ups subsided and we more or less retreated into the confines of our own homes.

In that quiet time of relative isolation, I wrote my first book and became pregnant with my third child. When restrictions eased and we could spend limited time in open settings with our friends and loved ones, I was living under a blanket of fear backed by terrifying studies on pregnant women who had contracted early strains of Covid and the risks to both mother and baby. Cue more anxiety, more plot twists, more uncharted waters.

I stayed as cocooned as I could. Besides a friend I went walking with, I'm not actually sure that any of my friends saw me pregnant at all. That's nine months of living as a virtual recluse, in stark contrast to the full and active social life I had before.

After our beautiful boy was born I spent another chunk of time sequestered away, trying to keep the risk low for my little newborn. There was so much we didn't know about the virus and fragile little immune systems that were just beginning to develop. It just felt safer to limit my engagement with the outside world.

Those Covid years—with new patterns of remote-contact relationships and invitations I was unable to accept—became my new norm. My world shrank considerably.

When our little one was a few months old and the risk of Covid in the community felt like it had settled somewhat, I accepted an invitation to a friend's delayed 40th. It was a lunch event and all my school friends, who had been a big part of my life for more than two decades, would be there. I was nervous and excited, and felt like the new kid at school all of a sudden— with my oldest, dearest, closest friends. The difference was we hadn't been physically present in each other's lives for much of the previous year.

I felt like an imposter. I had been acutely aware of the lack of connection over the months prior, but also felt that I'd had to make decisions for my own safety and that of my little one that I wouldn't have even considered before. I had become accustomed to my new normal of working from home, writing and podcasting from home, very much ensconced in my very small world. There was a part of me that felt an imagined sense of judgement from others who might have been questioning why I wasn't attending parties when I was pregnant, or who thought perhaps I should be back out in the world when the baby was born. But in those early weeks of 24-hour feeding and waking cycles when I barely knew which way was up, and the very real fear about risks to our health, I had changed my priorities.

It dawned on me that, while I had been busy in my internal world, life had gone on as normal for my friends. They had continued to catch up and go to celebrations (when allowed); they were seeing each other regularly and were up-to-date with each other's lives. It hadn't occurred to me that the rest of the world would keep on turning while mine had stopped.

I had fallen behind.

The distance I had perceived between us during Covid and the months of baby bubble was real. The love was still very much there, and I had some beautiful conversations and moments of reconnection that day, but I felt a little bit like an outsider.

Everyone else had continued on in each other's pockets, invested in each other's thoughts and lives, while I had been wrapped up in my new chaotic world of three young children and a slower emergence from lockdown life.

How much of this was real or imagined, I'm still not sure. But the urgency with which I used to pursue time with my friends had diminished, and I felt like I had missed out on pivotal moments as a consequence.

In my head, I suppose, I had hoped that everyone else was feeling fragmented and disconnected, too—that it wasn't just me. So it was jarring to see that everyone else appeared to have carried on as normal as soon as they were able to. Not only was it jarring, it was painful to imagine that connections *could* carry on without me. As self-involved as that sounds, my world had become very narrow and with that, the blinders went on.

I was also in a very different phase of life to most of my friends. I was trapped (albeit voluntarily) at home with a new baby—plunged right back to the beginning again with feeding and changing and surviving those early days—while most of my friends were relishing their newfound freedom with children who were off to kinder and school.

There were lots of reasons why I was feeling disconnected, and it was hard to admit that some of it was my own doing. I had leaned too far into the seclusion and forgotten that we actually need to nourish friendships, just as we do our romantic relationships. I had taken my friendships for granted. The outcome of that was a nostalgic connection with deep-rooted love, but I had lost the intimacy that comes with daily or even weekly contact.

I still haven't admitted this to them—or probably really even to myself, until now—but I really, really miss the closeness of those friendships. I miss the sisterhood. I miss being part of an unbreakable bond forged over a lifetime of in-jokes and shared memories, of paths woven so tightly together that we shared every step. The connections are still there, undoubtedly, but we no longer dissect each other's every thought, behaviour, decision or hypothetical. We have our moments, but it's not as frequent as it was.

It feels like a loss.

And because of that, I have been actively reigniting these connections again. There have been dinners, birthday parties and, this week, I'm going to a friend's house for a drink on a school night. (Going out after bedtime? Unheard of!)

Stepping back into those relationships has been like going home. Being with the people who knew me before I even knew myself is nourishing in a way that no other friendship can be. It's special. We laugh and spout loud opinions at each other about everything and everyone, we lament and commiserate, collude and embolden each other in every aspect of the lives that we are exploring. It has reconnected me with a very important part of my being, and I'm so grateful that I have been able to walk back into those connections again.

When we have young children, their needs, the demands of work and our very limited energy supply often mean that we're no longer able to live that carefree existence that we are reminiscing and fantasising about.

Our social networks keep changing and evolving as our stages of life do, too. When we have children there is a natural widening of our circle to include the parents of our children's friends: the school and childcare parents who we see every day doing pick-up and drop-off, and at the endless weekend birthday parties. The landscape is constantly changing.

I hear this from a lot of my clients and podcast guests, too. It's happening in friendships everywhere. There has been a shift in the dynamic for so many of us in this post-Covid world. The fabric of our social networks has frayed, and we are out of practice and out of sync.

But like so many things in life, nothing is linear. We can repair, recover and rebuild our connections, despite the relationshifts we may have experienced. I see many of my clients relearning the skills of connection. In my case, it's been about making an effort to make plans, go to events. Say yes to things more frequently.

But there is a collective feeling of burnout in the community that we need to acknowledge. Frequent and unwelcome plot twists have been inflicted upon many of us over the last couple of years, with interest rate hikes and financial stress increasing in most households. Many things are now out of reach. The cost of living is astronomical, and this plays a huge role in decision-making around how and when we can do the things we love.

These uninvited intrusions into our daily lives have been devastating. Underpinning it all is the fact that we are still emerging from our socially restricted lives of the Covid years.

For many of the students I work with, the psychological impact of those years has been immense. Those formative years of practising social skills were wiped out before they even partially mastered them. Covid had a similar impact on the adult population, too, with the incidences of anxiety and depression skyrocketing.

Social skills are not something we are born with; they are finessed and fine-tuned over a lifetime. This is something I tell the young people I work with all the time. It takes practice. When you suffer your first friendship fire or heartbreak, you learn how to pick up the pieces and keep going.

To feel love and connection—and to feel accepted for who we are by people who celebrate us—are some of the most basic human needs. When we don't feel that love or acceptance, or we have lost it, it can feel like a deeply personal rejection or a dismissal of who we are.

The dynamics of friendships aren't only complex in the playground—they continue to be throughout our lives. I once talked with my colleague Sandra about this, and she shared that her female friendships had once been the most important connections in her life. When she and her partner separated, it set in motion a shifting dynamic that left her questioning everything she had ever known.

Even though it had been a reasonably amicable split, there were some jagged edges in the division of assets and custody agreements and the relationship quickly soured. As can happen, their closest friends felt compelled to choose a side. In Sandra's case, many of her confidants and long-term friends chose her ex-husband. This came as a terrible shock in the aftermath of her separation; it was collateral damage she had not even vaguely imagined she'd have to deal with. Not only was she suffering the obvious losses of the end of her nuclear family and the imagined future she had seen for herself, but she was also grieving the inexplicable losses of her closest girlfriends. It was a painful betrayal. The women who had held her secrets, had held her hand through the worst moments in life and had stood arm-in-arm with her as they watched their children grow had crossed the floor to the other side.

When I asked her which was worse—the breakdown of the marriage or the loss of her friendships—she answered that if she were completely honest with herself, it was losing her girlfriends. They were her family that she escaped to when her own family was all too much. They were the safe place she went to when she needed support, and to lose them felt heartbreaking on a level she had not experienced before.

She had assumed that her friendships were the rock-solid non-negotiables, the safety net that would always be there to catch her when she fell. The loss gave her a bitter outlook. She described becoming quite jaded and was, for the first time in her life, weighed down by a sense of hopelessness. It was one thing to feel rejected by her ex, but if even her closest friends didn't love her anymore, what hope was there for the future?

Part of her distress came from the unanswered question: why had her friends chosen to desert her? Equally it was having all of these big, messy, unresolved feelings that clung to her like an apparition, haunting her each day and night.

She allowed herself time to grieve and wallow in all of that pain and despair.

After some time, she realised that she needed to find somewhere for all of those feelings to go. To name them, separate them, unpack them and deal with them. So, she went to therapy.

When I started working with Sandra she was a bold, outspoken, confident woman who appeared very much in control of her life.

She was incredibly warm and likable, so it was quite a surprise to hear that she had been in such a dark place. She was a force to be reckoned with in our workplace. You would never have known she had been through so much hurt and heartbreak. It's not that she was masking or hiding parts of her story; she had just found a way to move through it so that it was no longer interfering with her daily life. In fact, the despair didn't appear to be present in her at all by the time I met her some years later. The woman I met had a positive and hopeful outlook. She got there by allowing herself to grieve the cumulative losses of her marriage, her family structure and those incredibly close friendships. Instead of struggling and resisting and staying in the fight, she conceded that she needed to accept these shifts in her reality if she wanted to move forward.

Acceptance is a strange way of describing this process. I feel weird about using the word, even in relation to my own life. I have had to *accept* that I have lost my mum and so many other important people in my life, but it doesn't mean I have to *like* it. Acceptance doesn't make the loss easier, and it certainly doesn't mean the grief vanishes into thin air. Acceptance is about conceding that this is where we are at, in this current moment in life: acknowledging the parts that are hard to swallow, and taking steps forward in spite of the pain we may be in.

Acceptance is a mindset shift that can take us from the pit of despair to feeling more hopeful and optimistic, despite the loss and pain.

For my colleague, it was also about pouring love back into herself. After feeling unlovable and unloved, she thought this was a good place to start. (I wholeheartedly agree.) She started doing things just for her: things she had wanted to try but hadn't had the time or hadn't been able to prioritise. Things that pushed her out of her comfort zone and gave her opportunities to meet new people. She joined a sailing club and a community book club; she took classes in Thai cooking and pole dancing. She rediscovered joy and filled up her cup in new ways, always following her own interests and curiosities. Fatefully, she adopted a dog who became her little bestie, flooding her with unconditional love. She became a regular at the local dog park, which is where she met her new partner, who was also single, exploring new things and ready to meet new people.

By shining the light inwards, she was able to slowly pick up the pieces and begin again. She started listening to that little voice that said, 'I'd love to try that.' Instead of putting herself last, as we so often do in our busy lives, she decided to become the ultimate yes-woman to herself.

The most fulfilling love and acceptance comes from within. We are just subconsciously conditioned to believe that it needs to come from the outside world. The external measures that we reach for—those unspoken signs of a rich and fulfilled life; the things that we use to tell ourselves that all is going well—are so often temporary. The relationship, the family, the house, the job, the status, the collection of friends—any or all of these things can change, and when they do, this can rupture our identity and self-worth. The way out of that is by finding love for ourselves, regardless of what's happening around us.

As much as we might want to resist rocking the boat, trying everything possible to avoid going through these terrible and painful experiences, they are inevitable in the choppy waters of a long life.

We can expect our relationships to change. Some will blossom and grow; others we will lose and outgrow. The value we place on our partner and friends will fluctuate over time. Some of those shifts will be unexpected, while in other cases we'll have seen them coming for a while. Sometimes the real growth comes from walking away from the relationships or dynamics that no longer serve us or have become unhealthy or stale.

In all the versions of myself that I've been, I have had to take stock and recalibrate my relationships as my needs and priorities have changed. We all have to learn how to weather the storms when they approach and figure out how to ride them out. As we can see in all these examples of seismic shifts and friendships that have morphed into something untenable, the only way through it is *through* it.

We can grieve and wallow, feel the sadness and the pain. If we're not happy with where we are at, we can take steps to change that—through self-love, by taking action and by asking ourselves about the goals we would like to achieve and the new people we would like to meet.

But like all seeds of change, this takes time. Sometimes these ruptures and deviations are thrust upon us without warning, and at other times there can be a natural progression or erosion of connection. A sudden or slow plot twist unfolding. Understanding what we want and need from our relationships and connections is no easy task, no matter which way we arrive at it. Our wants and needs can also change over time, so the kinds of friendships we might have had in our 20s will look very different in our 40s, and again in our 50s (I'm secretly manifesting that life will be brilliantly mine again at this age—older children, disposable income, extended holidays) and beyond.

But I don't think this is a bad thing. As long as we're continuing to grow and evolve, our relationship needs should too. If our friendships aren't growing with us, perhaps it is time to move on—and that's okay.

Like so many facets of our lives, nothing is meant to stay exactly the same forever. Finding a way to be okay with that is part of our life's work. And as our relationships with others ebb and flow, so too will our relationship with ourselves. Turning the spotlight inwards and questioning how we feel, what we need and where we want to go, is key to our lifelong quest for happiness and fulfilment.

THINGS TO CONSIDER

➤ *Don't be too hard on yourself if a friendship has fallen away. Even within our own families, the intensity and levels of connectedness will ebb and flow.*

➤ *Ask yourself: How can I channel my energy inward and nurture my own interests?*

➤ *Remind yourself that these ups and downs are part of life and although they might cause incredible anguish at times, there is always something beautiful on the other side—once you are ready, of course.*

➤ *Pick up new hobbies, try new things, be silly, get messy—but, most importantly, be open to exploring new connections and people that come your way.*

10

Mindset

Going through something colossal in our lives can be quite disorienting, and can lead us down a winding path of confusion. However, there does come a time in the process where we can begin to move alongside the grief and pain in a different way to how we did in the beginning.

In the immediate aftermath we're in survival mode. We're just getting through it in whatever way works best for us—one hour, one day, one night at a time.

Before long we (usually unconsciously) move into the maintenance phase. Here we have returned to the real world somewhat but we're still treading water. While we're forever changed we're living what resembles a more normal life again. Of course, we will continue to wear the fresh scars of our loss and will absolutely still have terrible, difficult days. But in this phase we have begun to feel our way into some more solid routines, behaviours and ways of thinking.

A little bit further down the line again, we might have the energy to start shifting some of the more persistent patterns of thinking that are no longer serving us well. Some of us are able to do this earlier on, but for others it will take time and distance from the event that has altered our course.

For some of us, the biggest shift at this time is in our mindset.

Have you ever noticed that automatic voice in your head that provides unwelcome commentary on everything you do in life? You know the one I mean. The one that lurks in the darker recesses of your mind, waiting for an opportunity to slither out and say, *Told you so*. The voice that reinforces all the terrible feelings that might be brewing when the chips are down.

All good villains have a heroic counterpart to spend eternity in battle with—like Voldemort and Harry; the Joker and Batman. Unfortunately, when we're in the throes of distress, it's often the villain who is the loudest.

I notice it particularly when I'm having a bad day, when everything feels like it's going wrong all at once. It cuts in when I'm feeling overwhelmed, or when I need to be in a thousand places at once. Then I'll trip on something, bang into the door-frame, drop my phone or the shopping—whatever it is—and the automatic voice booms: *Great. Of course that happened.*

I could be racing to get the boys ready for school and can't find the drink bottle; then one of the kids is pulling off his socks again, and I can't find the lid to the lunchbox; then I discover another kid has gone outside and jumped on the trampoline, so his uniform is all wet. The dressing battle begins again. Finally, everyone, inexplicably, is ready to go. All are dressed, all bags are packed, all water bottles are accounted for, homework is in the bag, lunches and nappies and everything else is ready to go. Then as I reach the front door I realise I don't have the keys. I run back to the kitchen with three schoolbags on one shoulder and the baby on my hip, and I trip on a toy or knock over a glass of water. *Of course you did that/are running late/haven't even brushed your teeth. Because everything is hard. And everything always goes wrong!*

The voice also chimes in when I've had a professional knock-back and it feels like the straw that broke the camel's back. *That's it, I give up. There's no point anymore.* The instant negative narration cuts through without me even thinking.

In reality, it's never as conscious or directly spelled out as in the examples I've given here. I don't always hear fully formed thoughts or nasty barbs clearly spoken in full sentences. But the feeling is the same—it's an instant, recognisable feeling of *Oh, that'd be right* or *Argh, why does this always happen to me?*

Our automatic thoughts gang up against us the minute there is the slightest shred of 'evidence' to back them up. And usually, we believe what we hear. It's a psychological pile-on; confirmation that we might as well give up now, because everything is going wrong and there's no point trying to do anything about it.

The only evidence we usually need is one or two little things not quite going as planned, or a string of unfortunate events happening one after another. Or perhaps it's one big thing. Of course, when we've been through something distressing already, our resilience is low and so is our tolerance. In addition to the mental load that we might be carrying, perhaps we haven't slept well or are chronically sleep deprived. Our physical and nutritional reserves might be low. When you overlay the loss, grief, disappointment and perceived failure it becomes the perfect breeding ground for that negative voice to grow in size and confidence.

Plot twists are hard enough without the internal battle that can rage inside.

Our mindset can paint the picture of what the day is going to look like for us, how we will respond to things as they appear and what our mood might be like. From that negative place, every-thing is hard and confronting and the way out is unclear. We are bracing ourselves for the worst without even realising it.

It's quite easy to slip into a negative pattern of thinking, even if you're generally a positive-thinking person—especially when things have been tough. However, one of the best ways to move through the inevitable twists and turns of life is by reckoning with our mindset, and taking control of those thought patterns so they no longer rule us.

I'm not always a brilliant example of this, but I know some people who are. As you know by now, through my podcasts I have had the privilege of talking with so many incredibly brave, resilient and inspirational people who have experienced the worst that life can throw at a person. I've always been curious about how others move through unforeseen challenges and what it takes to make meaning out of the more difficult parts of life.

These conversations, as well as those I've had through my therapeutic work, make it abundantly clear that there isn't a single, one-size-fits-all solution to overcoming life's greatest obstacles. What I do know, though, is that we can all get there, one step at a time.

We don't need a special combination of blessed genes or grit from the gods. (Although some of that would undoubtedly help.) The truth is, for so many of the remarkable people I've spoken with, their way of coping and moving through unexpected plot twists has been about shifting their mindset.

Briony Benjamin is one of the extraordinary people who I have had the pleasure of talking with for both *The Curious Life* and *The Days That Follow*. Her outlook is awe-inspiring. She's one of those magnetic, radiant, light-filled people who seems to have a knack for shining a new perspective on things, even in the darkest of times.

When Briony was 31, she was living a thoroughly thrilling life. She had a fast-paced, thriving media career, a partner and a booked-up and busy schedule. Despite all the good things going on in her life, she could not shake a feeling of pervasive tiredness she had been experiencing. She described it as constant exhaustion, but thought maybe it was just the way adulting was *supposed* to feel. Feeling zapped and depleted, Briony pulled back from all her activities and consulted doctors—but no one could find anything wrong with her.

For over a year, Briony lived with this constant, overwhelming fatigue that permeated every part of her life and began to cloud her joy. She would find herself getting sick very easily and was always fighting off viruses. Her partner remarked that she had, in fact, been unwell for the entire time they had been together. Her symptoms then started to escalate. She developed a persistent cough, began to break out in hives and for three months was suffering with terrible night sweats that would leave her soaking in the morning.

Her parents insisted that she make an appointment to see a haematologist, suspecting something a little more serious than just the busyness of a successful life. And they were right. After a scan and some blood work, Briony finally received a diagnosis: she had Hodgkin's lymphoma. And in that moment, everything changed. Her entire busy, fabulous, burgeoning life came to a sudden standstill.

Mindset

Instead of planning the next shoot as head of video for Mamamia, Briony was mapping out immediate fertility treatments and chemo schedules. It wasn't anything she had any control over—she was suddenly, literally, in the fight of her life.

Early on, Briony's mindset shifted into a positive place. She recognised early that blaming the doctors or asking the universe why this had happened to her was wasted emotion and energy. Instead, she asked herself how she could get through this as lightly as possible.

That's not to say that she fell into the toxic positivity trap of thinking 'everything's amazing and I'm going to smile my way out of this'. With the support of a psychologist, Briony realised that it was okay for this entire situation to completely suck. She didn't have to like it, but she didn't have to completely shut down either. In her own words, she realised that you can't polish a turd—but you can roll it in glitter.

Sticking with the theme, she asked herself, *How can I make this less shit?*

She did that by rallying a team around her. She gathered up a support crew of friends and family members, counsellors and psychologists. She accepted that this was the place that she found herself in, and within that looked for something to be grateful for every day—even just the tiniest, most insignificant thing. She learned to experience the joy of missing out instead of the fear of missing out.

Instead of listening to that negative nagging voice that pulls us down and prevents us from moving forward, she worked on building her resilience muscle and took each day and each step as it came.

A positive mindset can propel you up and over the hurdles in life that you'd otherwise trip over on the way to wherever you're going. But what I love about Briony's message is that it's not about hyperpositivity or pretending everything is wonderful when it isn't. A more helpful mindset is where we acknowledge what is happening, how we are feeling, what we are going through, and then add in some lightness to offset the shade. This puts us in the habit of counteracting those negative cognitions—and the more we do it, the more naturally those positive thoughts become our go-to. Our brains start rewiring to automatically seek out the good things, rather than leap head-first into the negative.

Another inspiring conversation I had was with self-love queen Ariella Nyssa. She spoke of the darkness that she had blossomed from following a lifetime of people pleasing and living for others.

Ariella grew up in a very religious Christian community where the goal was to get married and have a family. When she was seventeen she met a boy and they began dating in a wholesome Christian way. Ariella was still very much committed to her faith, even though her parents had pulled away from it somewhat. She was attending Bible study, going to church, doing youth leadership—she was completely invested in her beliefs.

Mindset

Soon after graduating from school at the age of eighteen, Ariella's boyfriend proposed to her. She had reached the pinnacle of everything that her church groups had led her to believe she was working towards. She was achieving success, the way that it had been impressed upon her for so many years. A little part of her felt strange about it, but she leaned on her faith and said yes. Within six months, Ariella was married.

On the day of her wedding, Ariella started to panic. Her whole body entered fight, flight or freeze mode, her warning system screaming at her from the inside. Without knowing what was really happening and with the support of her father, she shook off the anxiety and walked down the aisle to be married.

In the months that followed, Ariella realised she wasn't happy. She started seeing a psychologist, who helped her begin to understand some of her patterns of behaviour. Most importantly, she helped Ariella give herself permission to say no for the first time in her adult life. Ariella had spent so many years people pleasing and saying yes to all the things, while disregarding her own needs and wants.

Bravely, Ariella decided to end the marriage and put herself first, for the first time.

What followed was a persistent barrage of abuse from people in her church, harassing her through phone calls, emails and on social media. Older people with authority, leaders and community members all told her that God hated her and that what she was doing was wrong.

What she was doing was making an independent decision in support of her own mental health. What they saw was somebody breaking ranks and not toeing the line.

Her self-love plummeted to an all-time low. She lost family and friends. Things became so dire and so distressing that Ariella attempted suicide twice.

When I asked her how she moved through that, she said she started listening to the little voice in the back of her mind telling her that she *was* worthy and she *was* enough, and that this pain and this time would pass. That's what brought her out of that dark and difficult place. During that time, her mindset shifted, and her inner dialogue became stronger. She would tell herself, 'I am not a victim. I am a strong woman. I can make my own choices.'

Gradually Ariella changed her own narrative, pushing the negative influence of her former community aside and building up a toolbox of phrases that helped her to transform her outlook.

By practising this shift in thinking and using her words and feelings with intention, Ariella was able to build herself up again to a place of self-love and self-worth.

The power of the inner voice never ceases to amaze me. It catches me off guard, too. You can know all the tactics and understand what you need to do to combat these mind ninja booby traps, but putting this knowledge into practice is what actually makes a difference.

Just like Ariella experienced, it's all about the repetition and the practice. It's accepting that as human beings we make mistakes. We don't always do things perfectly; we're not always going to get it right. Things will happen that trip us up and make us fall. But reflecting on those stumbles is what helps us to grow. Instead of breaking ourselves down with negativity and piling on with the insults and shame-mongering, we have to become good at taking stock and considering how we can do things differently in the future. We can choose to become victims of our circumstances, or we can actively choose to work towards the other side.

That is a mindset shift all in itself: transforming our perspective from a negative to a positive.

The thing to remember is that none of us actually nail this mindset shift all of the time In fact, aiming for constant positivity is completely unrealistic and unhelpful. Knowing, learning and practising the conscious switch out of one mindset and into another is an important skill to acquire. However, no one ever masters it to perfection. I'm sure Briony and Ariella would tell you that even today, there will be times that they have to work that little bit harder at a positive outlook and healthy mindset.

Each new situation, together with the layers of complexity around what might be happening in life at the time, adds new dimensions and viewpoints to work with. No one is perfect. No one manages their mental health flawlessly 100 per cent of the time. No one manages their self-care, secures their boundaries or achieves a faultless outlook 100 per cent of the time.

That's kind of the excitement of life. There is always something to work on. While no one would willingly invite these plot twists into their lives—at least not the tough ones—we know that they are inevitable. Change is the only constant we can expect in our lifetime. Understanding that—and relieving ourselves of the pressure of having to always know exactly what we're doing and how to do it—is a huge part of unburdening ourselves and accepting where we are at.

And believe it or not, accepting that we're not always going to have the answers or do things perfectly, or even well at all, is another great mindset shift that supports us through those difficult times. It's like letting ourselves off the hook so we can just *be*.

Recently I was treating myself to a rare self-care moment in the form of a beauty treatment (cue: mum guilt, financial spend guilt, time I should be writing guilt), and my lovely beauty therapist and I started talking. She shared that she had recently left a long-term relationship that had become very toxic. She had made several attempts to end things in the past but, finally, the last try stuck. It wasn't until she broke away from that relationship completely that she could see with perspective. She began to seek out stories of other women who had been in equally controlling and harmful relationships, and find out how they had recovered from them.

Almost instantly, the fog lifted.

Early on in her separation from her partner, she made the conscious decision to take this as an opportunity for growth and to learn from her experience. We unpacked that a little bit during our conversation (an occupational hazard for both of us!), and she said to me, 'I realised that I could sit there and be miserable, looking at all the things I have lost or am missing out on, or I could choose to accept where I was at and do what I could to move through it.' And that's exactly what she did. She poured all of her energy and focus into her own personal development and discovered an entire world outside of the one she had known—a world that has continued to fill her with inspiration, motivation and opportunities for growth.

Again, that was a choice about mindset. My beauty therapist made a decision: to actively shift her mindset from victim to victor. That's not to say that everything was peachy or that, miraculously, nothing hurt anymore. But two things can be true at the same time: you can be in pain and feel loss and sadness while also making a choice to move forward. Moving forward doesn't mean we forget. It just means we progress to the next stage of our lives.

In this book we've talked about how important it is to feel the lows and acknowledge our real emotions—not just for our mental health, but for our physical health. The more we bottle up our feelings by burying them, avoiding them or shelving them for another day, the more damage they can do in the long run.

I often use a Coke bottle analogy with the young people I work with. Think of emotions as the liquid inside a Coke bottle. When we shake that bottle up, it's like what happens to us when we go through life's experiences. Those in the know will slowly and carefully release the built-up gas, one tiny twist of the cap at a time, to avoid being blasted with the Coke. If we don't do that slowly, with careful intention, it will explode all over us. The same can be said of our emotions. When we take the hits and experience the pivots and twists and turns that life throws at us, we always have an emotional response. We are shaken up. The things we feel could be good or bad—happiness, elation and joy or distress, grief and pain. The emotional experience of life is limitless. When we bury those natural responses, we are not dealing with them carefully or with intention. Next thing—*boom*—we're likely to explode all over the next unsuspecting person who pokes us the wrong way. Or we might internalise the eruption, creating little explosions on the inside that we will see unravel in physical or emotional responses down the track. The impact of these internal explosions on our physical and mental health can be extreme.

I suppose the challenge comes from finding a way to sit in those feelings without letting them conquer every part of you. There are so many ways to do that. Have a big cry, let it all out. Talk to others; share your thoughts and feelings out loud. Write them out in a journal. Write a letter. Write many. Exercise.

Scream. Go to therapy. Connect with a community of people who have had similar experiences. Connect with people you love, and who love you. Find ways to release the pain in a safe and healthy way.

Once you have found what works for you—and that may be something different each time—you can walk towards the thing that is causing you the most fear. This may be fear of the unknown, fear of what comes next, fear of being alone or fear of having to connect. Again, this will look completely different for each of us, each time.

Hiding from those feelings, and from the fear associated with them, will only act as a mechanism for that metaphorical exploding Coke bottle. It will find a way to disrupt your life again, and it can get pretty messy.

$\mathcal{Y}$

The American psychologist Carol Dweck believes we can have a fixed or a growth mindset. Those with fixed mindsets are often stuck in rigid or negative thinking that prevents them from moving forward. Having a growth mindset, on the other hand, means believing we can learn from our mistakes and our challenges, and that we can improve our situation over time. By developing a positive outlook and accepting our mistakes and perceived failures we can evolve past our pain. We can acknowledge that bad things can and may very well happen, while knowing that in time we can turn those situations into lessons to learn from and experiences to grow from.

In line with Dweck's theory, if we move towards a growth mindset that recognises challenges and difficulties as a way of learning and evolving, that is the very definition of turning our tragedies into triumphs.

If a growth mindset is something new to you, consider how you might begin to challenge your current narrative. Being selective with your thoughts and careful with what you're telling yourself is a good start. Again, it is absolutely not about toxic positivity or having to remain upbeat and joyful all the time (it never is); it's about acknowledging what has happened and encouraging yourself to move forward.

It's easier said than done sometimes, and I am definitely no shining example when it comes to self-talk and mindset. Like many, I can fluctuate between gratitude and positivity, and negative spirals and a grim outlook.

The key, I've found, is to let ourselves off the hook when those pits occur or when we find ourselves falling back into bad habits. It's recognising when our self-talk has become negative and changing gears. It's reminding ourselves that this is one moment in time on a particularly difficult road that we're on right now— but that, in time, things will improve and we will find our way again. Those little modifications in the way that we think and talk to ourselves can make a big difference to how we feel about ourselves and our place in the world.

Just knowing that we have the ability to shift our perspective and move towards better days is sometimes all the magic we need to keep going. So, if you feel that old villain, that negative narrator, creeping in from the corners again, just remind yourself that you are doing the best you can under these circumstances and send that guy back where he came from. Nobody needs that kind of negativity when they're just trying to put one foot in front of the other. Bring out your inner hero and give yourself a much-needed mental hug.

THINGS TO CONSIDER

➤ *Ask yourself: Does my mindset need a shake-up?*

➤ *Take an inventory of the kind of self-talk you're using daily. Clock each time you have an automatic thought that sounds like discouragement, rather than encouragement. Make a note of these and then reflect over the list after a week or so. Notice any patterns of thought emerging. Do you commonly have negative responses to certain situations?*

➤ *Actively try to replace the negative with a positive—something that is supportive and encouraging, the way you might speak to a friend. Look for ways to negate the automatic thoughts* with a message that builds you up, rather than pushing you down.

➤ Remember that you have survived something huge, and you are still surviving. This is not the end of the road, it is just the beginning.

11

Arrival Fallacy

I'm always half-joking about my eldest child being born in a hurry and never having slowed down since. I'm a bit like that, too. I don't have nearly the same energy as he does in a physical sense, but I'm always pushing myself on to the next project, the next venture, the next chapter. I'm constantly seeking the next challenge and the next experience, assuming that's the natural progression towards wherever it is that I'm going. It's rare that I'm ever just sitting in the 'now' of my experience, without my brain scrambling for 'what's next'. It's pretty exhausting actually, but as a passionate and curious person, I'm never really satisfied with what I have going on at the time. I'm always on the hunt for the next thing. I'm always trying to get 'there'. But what that mythical place is, I don't actually know.

If I look back on my journey so far, the 'me' from five years ago would be thrilled with where I am today. Even the ventures that I've tried and failed at are things I would be patting myself on the back for giving a go. But I wonder what it will feel like when I think I'm 'there'. Will it be that I've achieved the next level of income, that more of my projects and ideas have come to fruition? Will I be on a completely different career path than what I'm currently doing? The truth is, I don't actually know.

Even as I near the end of the writing process for this book, my brain is already workshopping granules of ideas for what I will write next. I suppose it's the downside of having many varied interests and the motivation to try new things: I'm chasing a fantasy that keeps my brain busy and my schedule full, with an imaginary end point I'm moving towards.

From hearing the stories of many well-known and impressive people I have learned that not everyone is satisfied when they have reached what others might consider the pinnacle of their career. They feel dejected when they realise reaching their biggest goals hasn't actually reduced their pain, improved their mental state or quenched their thirst for advancement in life.

When we're in a low point in our recovery from loss, we often fantasise about the idea of getting to the other side. We think that one day, we'll make it through the worst of it (we do!) and that we'll be able to look back on all of our pain with relief that it's over (we will!). Of course, that doesn't mean we think we will never feel pain about the loss again. We're just chasing the fallacy that 'there' will always be better than 'here'.

For many of us, that golden hope that one day we will get 'there' is what keeps us going. What we have to be careful about, though, is focusing all of our energy on the magical 'then' while missing out on living in the now. (Take note, Jana.)

These days, more than twenty years since I lost my mum, I certainly have enough distance that I can look back over those awfully dark and painful days and honestly say that I'm out the other side. Of course there is still sadness. There are still moments that sting with the injustice of all that I have lost, and the wonderful things she is missing out on. But I've integrated my pain and the loss into my new normal. It lives within me and beside me, but without consuming me anymore. It did take time; a long time. But in the most recent years, I haven't noticed the work at all. My recovery has just been ticking along in the background, ensuring that I can live a productive and fulfilling life without feeling trapped or weighed down by my feelings. This is very much 'later' work, beyond the psychological first aid needed in the aftermath and the 'just keep going' of the maintenance phase.

In my first book, *Embracing Change*, I wrote about the closure myth that many of us feel pressured by in those early months or years following a loss. In a nutshell, the closure myth is the notion of striving to reach a certain point in our grief that will signify an end to our pain and suffering. This idea has gained popularity in pop psychology and found its way into the vernacular, selling us a false hope that one day, all the threads will come together and our loss will finally make sense. That as we make our way down the muddied streets of grief, finally reaching closure will give us the respite and reprieve we were looking for.

Unfortunately, though, as anyone who has been through grief or loss can attest, there is no closure point in grief. There is no magical date or event or circumstance that suddenly relieves us of the burden of our loss and sets us free and back out into the world. Hanging our hopes on the expectation that we will suddenly arrive at a specific point in our processing where every-thing will miraculously be okay is only setting ourselves up for more distress and prolonged pain. Because when we inevitably *don't* feel magically okay, the grief can become more complex and layered with guilt for not having done it 'right', or not having reached this mythical milestone that will set the world back onto its axis again. In blaming ourselves we can exacerbate our feelings of desolation and despair.

In my work I commonly hear people saying things like, 'I've put all of this time and energy into getting closure, yet I still feel exactly the same way as I did yesterday. What's the point? There must be something wrong with me.'

There is nothing wrong with you. You've just been sold the closure myth.

Arrival Fallacy

We hear about closure everywhere: in the movies, on TV, on social media. Everyone is seeking closure to make it all better. Perhaps somewhere along the way the idea of closure has been confused with seeking answers. If someone has passed away and we don't understand why, we naturally seek answers. If a relationship has ended outside of our control, again, our brains might go into an automatic resolution mode, trying to make sense of the senseless. That's not closure, though. Having answers can be useful in processing our pain and loss, but it doesn't make that loss go away. Our loved one is still gone, and the grief remains. We might just understand more of the bigger picture or have some of the missing pieces to the puzzle.

The pressure that we put ourselves under to reach an end point is partly due to how much pop psychology has entered the chat through mainstream and social media. We see its effect in well-meaning memes and posts and out-of-context quotes. If you're following anyone on Instagram who is peddling the closure myth—unfollow immediately. You will feel better almost instantly and no one needs that kind of pressure in their lives! Although I'm sure it's well intentioned, it's unrealistic to be moving towards an untenable goal where we believe a certain timeframe or milestone will set us free. Life and loss can be hard. But there aren't too many shortcuts through the tough stuff.

Life's plot twists are challenging enough to work through without adding unreachable expectations to aspire to.

My friend Hailey recently went through a rollercoaster of a relationship, with highs like mountain peaks and lows as painful as the deepest grief. Despite many blow-ups and agonisingly slow breakups, they continued to find their way back to each other over and over again. Even when they had both vehemently insisted that they were over for good that time, they never truly were.

When the end finally did cement itself in their reality and the rocky seas of their tumultuous relationship were still, Hailey began to experience the separation in a new way. For the first time she allowed herself to explore the loss with some finality and began to do the work of discovering who she was as a separate entity. We chatted during that time and she would share where she was up to in her exploration and her grief. She took to this search for answers with a fervour I hadn't seen in her before. She was wildly passionate about understanding the patterns of behaviour that had led her back into this relationship each time. She was diving into therapy and the theories of human behaviour from every angle. While this is a noble endeavour, and one that I thoroughly endorse, it soon became clear that Hailey was actually veering off into something else—something that didn't seem to me like a healthy exploration anymore, but a version of void-filling that didn't sit well with me.

She started trialling various forms of therapy, and I noticed that she was starting with a new therapist every few weeks or so.

The red flags started waving frantically at me. It was like she was doctor shopping, which I understood all too well from my time in child protection and at the Coroners Court, but this was my friend. Instead of hunting for prescriptions, she appeared to be on a tenacious quest for *something*—but I couldn't work out what it was.

I was genuinely curious as to why she had leapt into this frenzied approach, and I asked her what she was hoping to achieve. Knowing that therapy takes time—that we must build the rapport and trust needed in the relationship to do meaningful work—I wasn't sure what she was aiming for. When she replied, her answer was very simple: 'I just want closure.'

Then it hit me: *Of course.* She was madly rushing from therapist to therapist, trying new styles and approaches to therapy. She is a goal-oriented person who is used to seeing success through her achievements. She was chasing that imaginary goal of closure: an end point that she thought would pluck her out of her pain. In her mind, it was just a matter of finding the right therapist, or the right therapeutic approach, that would act as a magical panacea to make all her misery melt away. She just had to find the right person and do the work—which she was ready and willing to do. But she was looking for the express lane, to zoom past the hard parts and find the last check box to tick off. Unfortunately, this meant that she was swimming against the tide. She was working relentlessly to move herself forward, but in reality she was chasing an unattainable goal that was taunting her from a distance.

She had been sold the closure myth.

It felt especially cruel seeing her working so earnestly towards something that didn't actually exist. We started to have some conversations around therapy being a place to do all that exploration, but that it was more about integrating her loss over time and building her relationship with herself. *That* was what would help her to feel like she had moved past the pain points. 'I just want to be over it,' she said.

In her successful life in business, Hailey moved in a binary world where there were clear goals and directions and key performance indicators that showed her exactly where to go to reach an end point. You can't really blame her for trying to replicate that in her personal life—set the goal, tick the box, move through to the next step. But emotions don't really work that way. Neither does heartbreak.

Not having a specific end goal to reach doesn't make the journey less important. We just need to recalibrate and rewire our understanding about where we are going.

It's okay to want to feel better—in fact, I *hope* we all want that for ourselves. But that single magical milestone where it all clicks into place just doesn't exist.

There's another theory, coined by Harvard-trained positive psychology expert Tal Ben-Shahar, called the arrival fallacy.

In his own words, the arrival fallacy is the illusion that once we 'make it'—once we attain our goal or reach our destination—we will reach lasting happiness. It's a concept I am very familiar with.

Much like the closure myth, thinking that there is a final destination we're shooting for creates a false sense of security. It's a false hope that propels us forward, only to be disappointed when we realise that our feelings come with us, too. There's no magic escape hatch. There are always more mountains to climb.

It can feel especially unfair if, like Hailey, we're busying ourselves with work—like therapy or self-reflection—that *feels* like it's helping us move towards a goal, but that in reality is based on a false hope that we can tick the boxes and be done with it.

Therapy and doing the work *works*, but it's not as simple as completing a list of tasks or doing our homework and, voila, we're fixed. It's about giving ourselves the time and tools to integrate the loss into our lives, so that we learn to live alongside it in a more cohesive and less disruptive way. The key is allowing ourselves the flexibility to ebb and flow with our feelings, and understand that we may take one step forward and two steps back for a while.

The flipside of the arrival fallacy is what happens when we get stuck. Getting stuck in pain or loss is another very real experience for so many people following a big life shift. When we go through something big, like a death or the end of a significant relationship, we can become tethered to that spot emotionally.

It is not a conscious decision; in fact, most people won't realise they've been in a psychological vacuum until they come out of it.

For some, the stuck place might feel like a safe haven: a place to avoid the hard stuff. This is an unconscious avoidance that is filled with everything else but what we probably should be doing to take steps forward. It can look different depending on the person, ranging from obvious life avoidance via excessive drinking and partying, over-sleeping or becoming stagnant, to simply having what looks like a busy and full life. Either way, there's very little progress forward.

There are people in my life who have been through colossal changes, and while their worlds have seemingly moved on, they feel anchored to that time and space where they were hurt. Instead of pinning their focus on an eventual future happy place they are unable to let go of the past. They're emotionally trapped in the aftermath of their loss, even many years down the track.

We may not have any say in the events that happen to us, but we do have the power to decide how we are going to embed the experiences into our lives. For example, if we're stuck, we can actively choose to move ourselves forward by going to therapy or starting work on our mindset and outlook, among many other things. We can decide that we want to feel different and be more engaged with our recovery and take steps to action that.

When we choose to remain in the lowest ebb of our pain, avoiding the work, avoiding forward motion, we are punishing ourselves instead of supporting ourselves. An unconscious sabotage.

One of my podcast guests, and someone I connected with on a deep level almost instantaneously, is the lovely Chezzi Denyer. She is very vocal about doing the work and seeking support when it's needed, and I really admire that in her. Chezzi is a producer and a mum of three and hosts a hugely successful podcast with her husband Grant called *It's All True?*

We had a deeply insightful conversation about her late-in-life ADHD diagnosis, and her courageous struggle with postnatal anxiety following the birth of her first daughter. That birth experience was incredibly difficult for Chezzi and resulted in a lot of pain and damage to her body. In the days and weeks that followed she became highly anxious. She couldn't sleep and felt quite manic at times. Although she couldn't clearly articulate it at the time, Chezzi knew that what she was feeling wasn't right.

As we've discussed in previous chapters, a new baby creates huge upheaval in any new parent's life—but this was different. Chezzi reached out to professionals for help and began a long journey of seeking therapy with psychologists, psychotherapists and counsellors. She even took things to the next level by going to a treatment centre overseas that specialised in PTSD.

Following her traumatic birth experience, it became apparent that all of the trauma she had witnessed as an early career journalist—attending accident scenes and seeing truly horrific and indescribably distressing things—had bubbled up inside her. She had become quite good at burying these horrifying firsthand memories and disassociating from the difficult feelings they brought up. But these traumas were reactivated by her experience of giving birth to her daughter.

It was deeply confronting for Chezzi to face her old traumas head-on while also undergoing the enormous transformation that occurs in new parenthood. Going through this experience gave Chezzi a new perspective on just how powerful the protective mind can be. To her credit, she chose not to disconnect from those feelings any longer and learned to face them. She dove into reading, exploring, educating herself and learning about others' experiences. She learned how to get into those difficult feelings and work through them instead of supressing them.

That knowledge was a gift. Although it was a lengthy process and hard work at times, Chezzi can now share her story openly and sit alongside the painful memories and experiences that she has lived through.

The difference between my friend Hailey's recovery and Chezzi's is that Hailey had a singular goal based on the inaccurate belief that she was hurtling towards a magical finish line where she would be 'fixed'. Chezzi, on the other hand, was doing the work with the intention of integrating those many layers of trauma so she could live with them.

It's not just in grief or loss that the notion of closure or the arrival fallacy can play out. In so many instances, we imagine that getting to a certain place in life will be like finding a pot of gold at the end of a rainbow. Once we've found that pot of gold, though, our automatic go-to is, 'What's next?'

While writing this book I have thought so many times, *If I can just get x amount of words on the page today, I'll be happy* (okay, admittedly that actually *does* do wonders for my mood). I often think once I finish this thing or reach that goal I'll be satiated. But instead I find myself automatically scanning my brain for the next thing to sink into. The next project to tackle, the next new venture to explore.

My focus and my energy are fixed on something in the future that I'm scrambling to get to, rather than doing the living of now.

When the wheels fall off, many of us clamber to get them back on without actually doing a deep dive inwards to understand how and why they fell off to begin with. I'm certainly guilty of that at times. It's much easier to bury our heads in the sand and resist the things that take time and energy away from our daily obligations.

But when we ignore those signs we disconnect from what our minds or bodies are trying to tell us—and they will *always* find other ways to get our attention. This can present as overwhelm, anxiety, depression, physical manifestations of illness or feeling run-down.

Just as Chezzi discovered, we have to get comfortable in the uncomfortable and throw ourselves head-first into our feelings if we want to move through them. It isn't always going to be fun—in fact, it rarely is—but eventually we learn that we can coexist with our pain and our loss. Instead of chasing what's next or the after, we can learn to simply be.

I'm hyperaware of the fact that I spend too much energy in overthinking and anxiety. It doesn't matter how much I know about balance and managing anxiety and stress, I only start to do something about it when it's too late. Usually it's when I'm already in that state and I'm madly trying to reel the anxiety back in. We could all do a lot more sitting in the *now*, rather than the *then*; this would help us disengage from a whole lot of that mental angst that comes with the scramble to rebalance from anxiety.

When big life moments happen, we tend to get sucked into a vortex of emotion and it can take a while to find our way back out into the air again. The more mundane disappointments and little burdens that come with everyday life can also take a toll. As they build up, we can lose significant energy focusing on the disruption to our lives, rather than allowing ourselves to move through it. But it's also important to remember that all feelings are okay and appropriate in the various phases of recovery. The further away we are from the impact of the plot twist, the more thought it's worth investing in where we are sitting with it all.

It's just like the power our mindset can have over our mental state. When we wallow in our failures or zoom in on what's missing from our lives, our energy is spent reinforcing that negativity and we manifest more of the same for ourselves. Negative goal setting—focusing on what you *don't* want to happen—it's a thing. Not only does that keep us stagnant, but it can compound our feelings and contribute to that feeling of being stuck.

In those times, we might need to refocus our energy onto something more tangible. Even if it isn't clear which direction to head in, taking an inventory and working out where it might be helpful to move our energy away from can be a good start.

In my conversation with author, astrologer and podcaster Jordanna Levin we got talking about burnout and energy distribution. She shared how, many moons ago, she had recognised where her own burnout was coming from. Jordanna described having been stuck in a toxic work situation as well as a difficult relationship. She was feeling exhausted, fatigued and, ultimately, burned out. She felt herself spiralling out of control in a physical and emotional sense and realised that something needed to change.

Upon reflection, she saw that what she was experiencing had a lot to do with her mindset and her energy expenditure. The first step for Jordanna was leaving her job. That's not always an easy step to take, especially if you have commitments and responsibilities, but sometimes (actually, at all times) your mental health has to come first.

After exiting the workplace that had been causing so much pain for her, Jordanna began changing her outlook and using her energy in a different way. She was able to recognise where she was using her energy in a way that was detrimental to her well-being, rather than being productive. Having the ability to shift her energy and mindset helped relieve Jordanna of the emotional and physical burnout she had been experiencing to start living a more balanced and fulfilling life. She chose to divert her energy in a more positive direction by exploring new avenues and taking steps to move forward.

We can choose to continue in a state or situation that doesn't serve us and isn't healthy, or we can choose to become unstuck.

If we are in an unhealthy workplace it can feel as though the magnitude of the situation is well and truly unsolvable. I have worked with clients in similar situations; I can see that all of their energy is being zapped by an environment that isn't good for them. But in that moment, stuck in the cycle, they have pinned all their hopes and energy on the 'one day' when their boss leaves, when they get a promotion or when they have saved up enough money to move on from the situation. That fabled arrival fallacy means they remain stalled in a terrible situation, waiting for the day to arrive when they're beamed out of it. Part of the work with these clients is to empower them to make clear choices about their present life, to redirect their energy into something meaningful and immediate. In other words, to address the problem in the now.

As we know, one of the biggest challenges in grief, loss and disappointment is the experience of being out of control. We don't have control over the people we have or don't have in our lives; we cannot control other people's reactions and responses. We can't always control our circumstances, either. But we have to keep reminding ourselves that we *do* have control over our own thoughts, outlook and direction in life. We must remember that we're not in a race to get 'there'. Instead we need to listen to our bodies, reflect on our thoughts and feelings and try (as hard as it can be) to be present. Even if that means things are going to get messy for a while. Wading through that messiness is *the work*.

THINGS TO CONSIDER

➤ *If you often find yourself leaping forward into the 'what's next' frame of mind, or you're straggling behind in the past, try some mindfulness activities to practise being in the present.*

➤ *Ask yourself: How can I stay in the present moment?*

➤ *Could you add in more walking, yoga or creative activities? Could you incorporate intentional practices such as guided body scans or meditation? There are endless examples of mindfulness activities available online, in podcast or video format— try a few different ones and see which ones you connect with the most.*

Plot Twist

➤ *Break the habit of living in fast forward or rewind. When you calm and quieten your mind, you reduce stress, anxiety and the challenges you face as a result of a plot twist.*

➤ *Trust the process and remember that you will move through it when you are ready to.*

12

Mental Health as a Verb

Most of the theories around resilience and weathering life's storms are based on the underlying concept of finding balance—ensuring we're doing what's needed to achieve or maintain good mental health.

The assumption is that our mental health is a fragile construct that we need to tend to and nurture, trying not to knock it off balance. But we are much more robust than that; in fact, I like to think of our mental health as an active, dynamic, full-bodied part of our being that we need to engage in the same way we would our physical health. That means not just waiting until we have fallen apart to implement the strategies that we know help us to feel well. We really should be filling up our cups, practising what works and identifying the tools that we like to work with best at all times, not just when we've been hit with a plot twist.

Part of our resilience is in getting back up when we've been knocked to the ground. Knowing that when bad things happen we will eventually pick up the pieces and one day feel like ourselves again. Giving ourselves permission to tread water for a while—this is part of the process as we're swimming our way to the surface again.

I was thinking about this as I greeted a lifelong family friend, Varun, who had recently lost his father very suddenly, followed by his father-in-law just a few short weeks later. Seeing him for the first time, I embraced him in a big bear hug and asked him, 'How *are* you?' He answered, 'I'm going to be okay.' I looked at him and replied, 'Yes, you are, look at me—I'm okay. But it's taken me twenty years to get here and genuinely say I'm okay. You do not need to be okay right now.' He smiled gratefully and agreed to give himself permission to *not* be okay in that moment.

There will always be things that knock the breath right out of our bodies, things that make us feel as though we will never recover. Resilience is all about the bounce-back. Even when we're in the depths of despair, if we have strategies in our survival kit, we can piece together the next chapter of our lives a little more cohesively.

There's this notion of being okay that I brushed across with my recently bereaved family friend. It's a strange one. It's something we aspire to be, that we're told we're going to be, that we feel pressure to be. But what is it to be 'okay'? Is it a state of living with the uncomfortable things in life, like death and loss, or relationships or careers we don't love? Is it the compromises and conceding we do in so many areas of our lives? Maybe it's the place we get to when we've resigned ourselves to the painful experiences that come with the privilege of a long and lucky life?

When we're not okay, does it mean we've stumbled backwards into poor mental health? Have we succumbed to the lows in life that we're socialised to believe are bad?

As you know by now, I'm a big believer in embracing all parts of ourselves. The lows are an important part of the multifaceted human experience. However, there are ways we can prepare ourselves for these inevitable pitfalls. We can give ourselves a leg-up so that when we do fall, we have the ability to pick ourselves up and bounce back to being 'okay' more easily.

One way of doing this is to look at our mental health as a verb.

Let's unpack what I mean by this. Mental health is not big, bad or scary. It's a state of being, just like physical health. We can be in good mental health or poor mental health, or somewhere in between. It's important that we remove any preconceived judgement about the state that we might find ourselves in.

When we've sprained an ankle and need some downtime to recover, do we shame ourselves for the injury? The difference between the way we judge and criticise ourselves for a mental health injury compared to a physical ailment is quite astounding. When we've found ourselves at a particularly low point it's usually because something has happened to alter the way we view ourselves or our place in the world. Is that something to be ashamed of? Absolutely not. Is there a way forward? Absolutely.

Thinking of our mental health as a verb—as an action word—is a preventative measure. Doing so encourages us to arm ourselves with understanding and strategies to manage those injuries when they occur.

There are the obvious things that we know about, things like self-care and balance, boundaries and connection. As I touched on in previous chapters, it might be that we need to say no to things more often to protect our energy. We might need to reorder our priorities and make more time for the things that help us to recalibrate and reset.

Another way to increase our mental health fitness is by spending time working out what actually makes us glow. Some people call this finding purpose; others think of it as seeking our calling or life's work. The trouble is, we don't always know exactly what that is or how to achieve it. When we dig a little deeper and unpack the true values we hold at our core—about who we want to be and what we would like to be spending our time doing—it is much easier to feel fulfilled and like we are moving forward.

When we have worked out the destination, the path becomes clearer.

But finding the path can be a little bit trickier when things haven't gone to plan, or when we're feeling as though our expectations have not been met because of the latest life diversion. It can create an accumulation of resentment, distress and frustration. When this happens, we can build up a wall and stop ourselves from moving through it—especially if this has happened before. If it's a heartbreak and you've experienced many before, it can feel like a mountain of negativity coming at you with the underlying message that you are undeserving of love. This is absolutely *not* the case. You are and always will be deserving of love and happiness. You deserve all of the good things in life; sometimes they just take a little longer to fall in place.

Finding a purpose can help move us towards that happiness we all deserve.

If you are clear what your purpose is, you can start taking steps towards it. Even though you may be grieving, you are still working towards something meaningful.

To be clear, you definitely won't feel like investing in a robust mental health strategy or making long-term goals in the beginning. This is part of the later work to do further down the track.

The feeling of being stopped in your tracks is part of the shock that comes with so many of these sudden plot twists.

But it isn't just the earth-shattering losses that can cause us to stagnate. The everyday roadblocks that are a natural part of life can create blockages throughout our life, too: things like not getting the role we applied for; having our ideas kiboshed in a meeting; feeling left out in a friendship; feeling unheard in a family discussion. These disappointments and setbacks happen across our lives.

Building up our resilience and giving ourselves a roadmap for bouncing back begins with understanding that these things can and will happen. The next step is to work out what is important to us.

I was working with a client, Maggie, recently on goals and purpose as she was feeling stuck in her professional life. Her work requires her to be creative and open to new ideas and ways of thinking. She had been flailing in recent months. She felt she had lost her drive and motivation for work following a long period of singledom and some complicated family issues. She didn't feel connected to her work anymore. It felt like she wasn't moving forward, that she had lost her mojo in every way. She had no desire to go out and meet people, the creative juices were drying up and she had lost her spark. She felt deflated and a bit lost.

After working through some of the layers of loss and challenge Maggie had been facing in her professional and family life, we decided to spend some time redefining the pillars of her value system. This would allow her to identify what her purpose and her goals were for the next phase of her life.

In a nutshell, our purpose is the place we want to get to, what we want to be. Our goals are the things we want to achieve, and what we will do on the way to reaching for those dreams. Doing this work gave Maggie a renewed sense of direction and sparked new energy within her. She was able to see herself as a whole person again, not just focusing on the parts of her that had not been going well. Identifying her purpose gave her a clear understanding of the *why* behind her drive to move into the next chapter of her life.

She identified creativity, independence, respect and empathy as the four pillars of her value system. Those were the values she felt most closely aligned with, the values that sustained her. Her purpose revealed itself as wanting to be creative in a useful and meaningful way.

This opened up an entirely new landscape for Maggie, giving her the opportunity to think outside the box and take leaps in her professional life that she had never considered before. Her goals gave her a new sense of direction as she moved towards a fresh destination. She found a way to combine her creative and people skills into a new business idea—fulfilling her need for independence and respect, which she didn't feel had been met in her previous role.

There were goals to set and achieve, reset and work towards, giving her a renewed sense of self, a clearer identity and a sense of excitement and anticipation.

Identifying the pillars of our value systems is imperative if we want to nourish ourselves from the inside. This is what fills up our cups. There might be more than one thing that's driving us intrinsically, and it can take a little time to work out what we align more closely with. Understanding our values gives us a backup plan to fall back on when things aren't going so well. If we work out what we value, then we can lean into that when we feel like we're losing control of the steering wheel.

Those pillars might include kindness, authenticity, balance or autonomy. Or they might include compassion, curiosity, flexibility or gratitude. The list is endless, and finding what you connect with will be an entirely personal experience.

When we know what we stand for and what is important to us, we have the clarity to refocus our energy on the things that make us feel good from the inside. When the rug has been pulled from beneath us and we find ourselves having to start again following a plot twist, this process can help bring clarity to the next steps.

I listened to the well-respected leadership mentor and life coach Ben Crowe share his thoughts on some of these ideas on the podcast *The Imperfects*. Ben is well known for his work with elite athletes such as Ash Barty and Dylan Alcott. He encourages his clients to ask themselves three key questions: *Who am I? What do I want? How do I get there?*

For some of us, finding our purpose can feel like an overwhelming concept. According to Ben, it's simply about listening to our intrinsic motivations and understanding who we want to be in life.

When we align our values with our goals and purpose, it's like a magic formula. When we deviate from our course—in the likely event of a life shift—it's okay, because we know where we're going. We can grieve and feel the pain of loss, rejection, fear, shame, whatever it might be, but then we tend to be much quicker to bounce back. We know what lights us up and what we need to do to find our way back to our values, purpose and goals.

If I drill down to understand what it is that I love doing—what makes me feel like I'm exactly where I'm supposed to be—it's not about writing books, creating podcasts or the therapeutic work itself. The bottom line is that I want to help people. That's what makes me feel like I'm doing what I'm *supposed* to be doing. The podcasts and the books and the therapeutic work are goals towards fulfilling my purpose—which is to help people.

That translates across all areas of my life, too. When I help someone in the supermarket, send a message of support to someone or genuinely thank a friend for a beautiful time spent together, it lights me up as it aligns with my purpose. I genuinely feel good about connecting with others on a human level. It helps me feel balanced and my cup is filled when I'm doing the things that make me feel good. That is part of the dance of maintaining good mental health, especially after taking the hits of the past.

Knowing that, I can focus on the goals that are aligned to my purpose. These include creating podcasts and having meaningful conversations with people; my training as a therapist and the work I have undertaken in the last eighteen years; and the deep conversations and connections I have with friends and colleagues that allow space for unburdening and debriefing when things are happening in our lives.

Understanding the things that throw us off kilter is also important in maintaining or returning to good mental health. Letting go of the things we cannot control is a good example of that.

The anxiety spirals that my family have become accustomed to usually happen when things feel out of control for me. Time and punctuality are inexplicably important to me. I'm sure this is a control thing: that being on time is part of an innate desire to control my external world. I am on time to everything, if not a touch early. When I was single I was always the first to arrive to a date. I would intentionally arrive a fraction early to scope out the location, choose a place to sit and be ready for the interaction.

Parties, appointments, arrangements of any type—I am always early or on time. I'm more than happy to sit in the car and wait out the five or ten minutes it takes for others to arrive because I can relax for a minute, knowing that I have found the meeting spot, have a car park and am ready to meet my friend, or whoever it is, at the arranged time.

This is just one of the ways that I worked out what is detrimental to my mental health (feeling out of control) and how I can manage it. I have no control over the person I'm meeting, how well the meeting will go or whether they will enjoy the interaction, find it useful or ever want to do it again. But to address my own anxiety (uncertainty), you can be sure I will show up early or on time.

If I am running late, it can feel like an enormous wrench in my outlook. My anxiety rises and my temper shortens just that little bit as I madly try to get through whatever the hold-up is as quickly as possible.

So you can imagine the source of much of our family stress. It's that feeling of being out of control. The mess, the noise, the beautiful chaos—it's all stress-inducing and fires up that part of me that wants to feel in control.

That's when the screaming mum lizard brain flies in and takes over the rational, getting-through-it mind.

The loss of control when you have a child is a universal experience. (At least that's what Instagram tells me; it could be my algorithm.) The things that trigger you when you're a parent have shocked and surprised me. I find myself regressing to a level of maturity that I last experienced as a kid myself. Tantrum mode activated! I become as dysregulated as my children can be in that moment. Our behaviours mirror each other's. When they are having a meltdown for some innocuous reason, my response is often to scream and yell in exasperation. The calm and rational grown-up evaporates into thin air, and the teenager masquerading as an adult takes over. When I'm tired, overwhelmed and feel pulled in a million different directions, the sensory overload is atomic.

In those moments, my reaction is usually completely out of proportion to the issue at hand. (Size of the problem, anyone?) It's usually because I have lost control, there is uncertainty and I am anxious—about getting to the thing on time, or trying to keep the house in some vague semblance of order. Or I'm over-stimulated by all the noise and visual chaos, and I can't take one more thing.

The first step in getting through this is recognising what I need in that moment. What does what I'm feeling really mean? It's usually about finding ways to feel in control, or needing a mental reprieve and some physical space from the problem for a moment.

This is important, because for me to manage my mental health when things happen that *really* matter, such as a death, loss, rejection, a career pivot or a relationship shift, I need to know what is going to help me stabilise and find my way back to some sense of normal. Of course, my responses to the daily battles of life are very different to the automatic responses to the big things that have happened, and I wouldn't expect to feel or react in the same way to both. But underneath most difficult situations is a feeling of loss of control, and needing to find some stability through it all.

Knowing what I need sits alongside the big feelings of loss, grief, pain or upset that have occurred. I feel them, own them, process them, marinate in them. And when I come up for air, even if it's just momentarily, finding a way to control some of what I can and let go of the things that I can't is what leads me to the next chapter.

Figuring out the things that work against us in crisis mode and the things that help to pacify us are also important actions to take in support of good mental health.

This brings us back to connecting with our values so that we can find alignment within ourselves. In a sense, it's about watering the garden regularly rather than waiting to get your plants into recovery once the storm has passed and left all the damage behind. It's about actively engaging in our mental health, practising the things that keep us well and balanced, even when life is good. Some of those things, such as mindfulness and gratitude, we have already touched on in previous chapters. These are activities that help us water the gardens of our minds.

I wrote about mindfulness and gratitude in my first book and have been interviewed about these ideas in the media. There's a reason that these concepts are becoming so mainstream now. It's not only because of the clinical evidence that demonstrates the effectiveness of gratitude and the neurological benefits of regular practice; it's also because it has been proven to increase happiness, improve health and wellbeing, aid in stress regulation and reduce negative mental health outcomes such as anxiety and depression.

Hugh van Cuylenburg of the Resilience Project is an advocate of the GEM model for good mental health and happiness. That is, practising *gratitude*—focusing on the things we are thankful for in our lives; *empathy*—thinking about the people around us and finding ways to connect with and support them; and *mindfulness*—finding ways to stop, find stillness and pay attention to what is happening now, in the moment. These three concepts can help us to rechannel our energy and focus on things outside of ourselves, which is an excellent practice to get into when we're flexing that mental health muscle.

We know these things work, but it's crucial that we practise them year round, not just when the big bad things have already happened.

I know the GEM model works for me, yet even with all of this research and evidence in the back of my mind, it's also something I easily fall out of the habit of. So don't beat yourself up if you're not in the regular habit of active mental health. Just take baby steps and find ways to encourage yourself to stick with it.

Last year I did an accountability exercise where I showed up on Instagram every day for seven days to publicly declare two things I was grateful for. I did it as a personal experiment to see whether I could really feel a difference in my outlook at the end of a very busy, very stressy new-baby-and-too-many-commitments kind of year. I began with simple things—whatever came to mind. But within a couple of days, I began to notice a shift in my thinking. I was starting the day wondering what it was I would be grateful for that day. Throughout the day I was noticing moments or flagging my reactions to things that I could tuck away for my gratitude testimony at the end of the day. Within two or three days, my brain was already rewiring itself to look for things I was grateful for, rather than ranting in my head or to my partner about all the things I was stressed and overwhelmed about. The practice was shifting my focus away from the negative and towards the positive.

By the end of seven days I noticed a marked improvement in my outlook. I intended to continue the practice into the following week, but the days got away from me and my enthusiasm for doing it on a public platform waned.

So I completely understand that some of these activities can be hard to maintain. But doing these practices, spending those five minutes a day—that's literally all it takes—to create a moment for ourselves and look for the things that we are grateful for, genuinely does improve our mental health.

They're good, healthy practices that support good, healthy minds.

It might feel overwhelming if you haven't given much thought to what lights you up and what gets in the way, but start small and work your way up. Gratitude, kindness and empathy inwards is just as important, too.

Improving our mental health when we're in the everyday mundane lanes of life is the juice we need to support our systems when things come crashing down around us.

THINGS TO CONSIDER

➤ *Ask yourself: What can I do to actively work on my mental health each day?*

➤ *Review your daily mental health habits. Prioritise them in the same way as you prioritise good nutrition, quality sleep and exercise for your physical health. What habits can you start today?*

➤ *Google a list of values and work your way through it. Create a triage system—important, not so important, not important—and start thinking about the values that leap out at you.*

➤ *Start sketching out what your purpose may be. It can take some time for this to become clear, so don't feel bad if it doesn't reveal itself in its perfect form right away. Play with the idea and think about how your purpose will align with your values. After that, goals should start to emerge that will set you on the path towards the next chapter of your life.*

➤ *As always, treat yourself with kindness and empathy.*

13

The Hidden Shifts

Sometimes we go through the deepest pain and anguish in *anticipation* of a potential loss, even before the worst has happened. We may have a child who is unwell or a loved one who is battling a significant illness. We may be living with a partner or a parent with dementia. We may have had a discussion with our partner about our relationship and found out one of us would like to work towards a healthy end while the other wants to hold on. These anticipatory moments can create enormous life interruptions. And the unravelling can begin at the first inkling.

The protracted anticipation of loss or pre-empting a change can have a significant impact on our lives. There is even a name for it: anticipatory grief. As the name suggests, it's a state of being that has us preparing for the worst before it actually happens.

Anticipatory grief usually occurs when there has been genuine cause for the process to start—it isn't usually about hypothetical changes. Knowing that someone you love may not be in your life for the long-term can be devastating in every way. The slow-motion decline towards the end of a relationship is a big one for many of us. There can be a knowing and a grieving long before the person leaves (or before you leave them).

For those of us who have been affected by grief in the past, pre-emptive grief can feel very familiar. It's almost as if our minds and bodies are preparing us to fight the big fight again, preparing us to go up against those old recurring feelings that we know are imminent. We're bracing ourselves for what is to come.

Sometimes it's an unhealthy anxiety that triggers those feelings to bubble up to the surface: a hangover from previous losses. It's a protective mechanism that's running a little bit higher than it needs to be. It is usually something that you have no choice in, when the situation is completely out of your hands.

Nearly a decade ago my beloved golden retriever Casper was in his final weeks of life. He had been by my side through the good and bad during those first eleven years after Mum died. He was my shadow and my true soul connection.

In the first year of my masters, when our ethics tutor asked us to bring to class something that was meaningful to us, it didn't even occur to me to think beyond my cherished companion. There was nothing else in my life that filled me with so much love, security and happiness. We were a package deal, and anyone who met us knew that. So, Casper came to uni.

Some years later, while my partner Chris and I were in Sydney for a weekend, Casper became severely unwell. Completely out of the blue—no warning, no signs—he was gravely ill. My brother, who was looking after him for me at the time, raced him to the out-of-hours vet. The phone call I received from the vet went something like, 'This dog has internal bleeding and is going to die today, unless he undergoes immediate surgery to find out what is going on. It's a lot of money, so make sure you're okay with your decision.'

The surgery would cost $20,000. The whole situation was completely unexpected in every way: just the day before, when I had kissed him goodbye to head to Sydney, he was a perfectly healthy and very happy dog. No dollar amount could have stopped me from saying to the vet, '*Yes*! Do what you have to do!'

My partner and I threw all of our holiday belongings back into our bags and hurtled down the highway towards Melbourne. It took what felt like an age. We drove through the night until eventually, the vet clinic called and advised that the surgery had gone well and we could take our time coming back. Casper would sleep through the night, and we could collect him in the morning.

Haggard and bleary-eyed from the urgent drive home, we pulled the car over to a safe place and slept for a few hours before continuing onwards.

My beautiful boy was diagnosed with hemangiosarcoma, a cancer of the blood vessels that is usually only diagnosed after an internal rupture when it's already too late. The vet advised that Casper had done well through the surgery but that the prognosis was not good. She said that most dogs with this condition only live on for another two to six weeks if they survive the initial rupture. In most cases, the cancer will have spread throughout their body and they cannot outlive it.

I was absolutely shattered. Casper meant everything to me, and I could not imagine a world without him.

It's striking how quickly our previous pain can resurface when a new loss emerges. It's as if the bruises from before are fresh again under the skin and there is an instant smarting of hurt. The desperation and distress that might have been simmering under the surface boils right back into consciousness, and there's a familiar feeling of dread that comes with it. You've been there before, you know how much it hurts and you don't want to go through it again.

Casper lived for another four weeks. After recovering from the surgery he was back to his usual self: happy, energised, playful and loving as always. I was lulled into a false sense of security, even though the vet warned me that I would know when he wasn't okay anymore and to prepare for it.

For the time being I tried to enjoy my sweet boy, but soon enough the anticipatory grief set in. It can feel like a deep fog, a haze of disbelief and despair that sits low in your belly. There is a hint of nerves around the edges as your brain tries to rationalise the situation, searching for loopholes to get you out of this state and rewind the clock back to before you had the distressing information. You look for signs that will tell you the medical professionals are wrong. You google the condition, searching for evidence that others have survived this before. You are grieving in all of the ways that you do when someone has died, except they are still there in front of you.

I clung desperately to every moment with Casper. I watched him like a hawk and made every kind of deal with the universe to keep my boy alive. None of them worked, though, and soon enough he was once again very, very unwell. Within 24 hours we had to make the awful, heartbreaking decision to do what was right for him.

Anticipatory grieving can serve a useful purpose. It can provide an opportunity to say the things you have always wanted to say, to prepare for a future without your loved one and to start doing some of the early internal work to somehow find meaning in these difficult and painful times.

On the flipside, it's important not to become stuck in a negative loop, spending vast amounts of energy in worry and anxiety that *one day* something might happen to the people we love. That kind of hypervigilance is what happens when the pendulum swings too far the other way. I can tell you from personal experience just how exhausting and useless that state can be. Having lost so many important people in my life, I do spend vast amounts of time and energy worrying about losing the people I love. Loss is inevitable, I know that. But I also know the place of loss so well and I love my people so much that I don't want to go there again.

I am aware that this worry is a complete waste of time and energy in my case, as it's not something that is even vaguely within my control—and we know how important a sense of control is to me!

I was talking with a friend about this. She said, 'You're going to grieve the people you love when they're gone anyway, so why start the process earlier than you need to?' While this statement is entirely accurate, it is easier said than done sometimes.

When we find ourselves ruminating, spiralling or holding on to our fears, this can be an indication that we still have some work to do on our original loss. Perhaps we have built up walls around that loss or buried ourselves in avoidance, causing us to react to new challenges in ways we never would have before. There is a lot of rewiring that goes on after a transformative experience and it can take some time to see where the new cables have connected.

Recently I was working with a client, Jodie, who had experienced several significant breakups, including an engagement that was called off and a long-term de facto partner who suddenly called it quits. Naturally the scars resulting from these losses ran deep and the burden she was carrying was heavy.

When Jodie came to see me she had cautiously entered into a new relationship, but she had one foot in and the other firmly out the door. She had built up a rickety little house of defence around her fragile heart in an attempt to prevent people from getting in and breaking it again. But her defences also prevented her from getting out.

Jodie was inventing new boundaries, new rules and new ways to test her partner. She held him at a frosty arm's length, defensive and tense, daring him to leave her. Because isn't that what they all do? They leave. That was her mantra at the time. But her tough act was smoke and mirrors. She would come to me sobbing and broken as though the relationship was already over and the worst had already happened. She was pre-emptively grieving the end of this relationship that had barely even begun.

Jodie was surprised to discover through our work together just how much she actually wanted the relationship to succeed. She had done such a good job of convincing herself that the breakup was inevitable, that loss was what she should expect out of life now, that she couldn't see how much of the good stuff was actually there. It sounded as though her new partner was very much invested in the relationship and had no intention of going anywhere—despite Jodie's many unconscious attempts to sabotage their connection before he could.

With time, and in doing the work to heal some of her past pain, Jodie was able to open herself up to the very real possibility of a future with her new partner. There would be occasional bumps in the road and moments where she might slip back into that protective mode that had been her go-to for so long, but the channels of communication had opened right up. She and her partner could talk about her sadness when it arose as she recognised that reactive dread rising up inside her. They identified it as a representation of her love for him: that she cared for him so much that she didn't want to lose him. By reframing the experience, and feeling safe enough to share it openly in the relationship, Jodie was able to integrate her previous losses and pain into her current experience in a healthy way.

We all come to new experiences with a whole life lived up until that point. Some of what we've lived through will be good, some of it won't be. Our past informs our behaviour and creates patterns of thinking, some of which we will turn into the narrative of our lives. We don't always see how our past experiences might be playing out in the current day. Sometimes it can take an outside perspective to draw our attention to it.

It's important not to let those past experiences colour our new lives entirely. If we did that, we would live in a constant state of fear and dread that isn't good for any of us. (Hello, anxiety.) Our hurt will eventually dissipate, but we might need a little nudge to ensure our past pain doesn't become the dominating force in our next chapters.

Starting something new can be scary. There are fresh feelings and situations to tackle that we might not have had to face in our recovery state. Sometimes that might send us running in the opposite direction of growth and new opportunities. But when that happens, we're not really living. Hiding can only serve us for so long; after a time it causes us to stagnate in avoidance.

When you notice that your past is bubbling up to the surface, know that you can do something about it. Nothing is fixed, nothing is permanent. You don't have to be defined by your past or the things that have happened to you or around you. You have the power to change your thinking and behaviour and extricate the hidden patterns over time.

As we move through the recovery process there are so many little shifts that occur within us. We might not even be aware of these until we stop to reflect on where we're at.

Struggling through the mass of emotions in the early aftermath of a plot twist takes up so much energy and brain space. It's not a choice, of course; it's a matter of survival. Our brains do so, so much work in this time. It's exhausting; the burnout and fatigue are extreme.

In the middle years, the maintenance phase, we have more space to allow other parts of our lives to open up again. We have a little more energy to do things outside of our grief, while also managing to cope with the emotional distress and physical loss that's continuing to recalibrate in the background.

In the later years, when our brains and our emotions have settled into a more stable place, the energy we have for life far outweighs what we need for our grief. In that phase, we can look back at how far we have come and articulate some of the hidden shifts that have taken place within us. There is much to be learned through this process.

Some of the later-years reflection comes from the way that we learn to tell our story. We create a narrative around what has happened to us: what the experience was like, how we felt, what we did, how we survived it. We choose to share the parts of the story that were most meaningful. Our distance from the event means that we are able to do this with less distress and emotion than in the beginning.

We are the authors of our own stories. Through each experience, we gain the tools and insights we need to shape our next chapters. It won't feel like it in the beginning, but in the later years we can take control of the narrative that we create for ourselves and decide what our experience is going to mean to us.

We can choose to be a victim of our circumstances, or we can choose to have survived something truly terrible that has changed us in every way. The language that we use and the emphasis that we place on each experience will dictate what it means for us in the landscape of our post-grief, post-loss life.

I can talk about my experience through incredible grief. I can reflect on the subsequent losses and the pivotal relationship breakdown that I went through at that difficult time. I experienced a huge amount of change and loss and nothing will ever make it better. That my mum isn't here to celebrate and support me through my adult life is heartbreaking. I would give anything to have her be a grandmother to my children. They are missing out on a real-life connection with one of the most special human beings who ever existed, and who I was lucky enough to call my mum.

But I am choosing not to be permanently damaged by my experiences. I try to notice when I'm being triggered to respond to current-day events in an unhelpful way due to what I have been through. I can identify and articulate the parts of myself that have changed and why I might be reacting the way I am, and acknowledge what I'm feeling as a hangover from the past.

It never, ever means that I am 'over it'. We will never be 'over' those huge and irreparable losses. But I am in control of what it means to me, how I share it and how I bring those experiences into my future.

I wear my scars proudly. I know that I have great strength and resilience within me, born out of necessity. I don't want to have to rely on them again any time soon, but I know that these qualities exist in me in the spaces that were not there before. I know that I have a much greater understanding of the hardships of life and that I can genuinely connect with others who might be going through their own experiences of loss or distress. That is something that has manifested within me as a result of my own pain.

It's one of the hidden shifts that have happened because of what I have been through.

It might not feel like it yet, but one day you too will be able to look back on the path that you have walked and acknowledge how far you have come.

Every story has a beginning, a middle and an end. When one chapter closes the next one opens.

Whether we are anticipating a loss or have been through something sudden and unexpected, there will be changes taking place inside us that we may not even be aware of yet. Accepting that change is inevitable, and that loss is part of our story, are important parts of developing our new narrative.

But although it's part of our narrative, loss doesn't define us and shouldn't prevent us from moving forward. When we are ready, we will find a new voice to re-author our story to create a narrative that we are comfortable with—one that aligns with the hidden shifts and changes that have taken place within us as a result of our experiences.

Wear those changes with honour; be proud of how far you have come. Even if it has felt like you're taking tiny little micro-steps forward at times, you are here today and you have an important story to tell.

One day, you will feel empowered telling the story of what you have been through or are going through now. It definitely won't feel empowering right away, but in time, it will.

As with everything in recovery, this requires time, patience, kindness and plenty of love for ourselves.

THINGS TO CONSIDER

➜ *There will be changes that are continuing to unfold as you get further down the road from your plot twist. Reflect on the last six months and check in with where you are at. Can you identify any of the hidden shifts that have unfolded without you noticing?*

➜ *Ask yourself: What are the different parts of my story and how do I want to tell them? Write out the beginning, the middle and the end of your current chapter. What will your next chapter look like?*

➜ *What steps might you take towards that next chapter? You are in control of the next phase of your life, armed with new skills, such as resilience and strength, that you might not always believe are there. Remember, you are making progress even when it doesn't feel like it.*

Conclusion

There are always things we wish we had done better, learnings we mentally store away for 'next time'. But the truth is, we can't always predict the intensity of the feelings that will come up when the next thing hits—even if we feel better prepared from a logical perspective.

Yet I hope that this book has impressed upon you that feelings are nothing to be afraid of. Lifting the lid on them won't release a beast that cannot be tamed again. Every emotion is a valid and important part of the human experience.

The grief we feel after a loss is an expression of how much we loved someone or something; how much hope we had attached to that part of our lives; how much of ourselves we had invested in that time.

I really do believe that all of the things—the good, the bad, the messy and the hard—lead us to wherever we are meant to be going.

Some of it can feel desperately unfair and inequitably apportioned. But having been through pain before, you know that you can, and you will, come out the other side.

Even as I have been writing this book I've had new little twists to navigate. During the past months my father sold our family home in a lightning-fast transaction. We didn't have too much time to think about it. Since then, we have been through the process of sorting and clearing a lifetime of memories. I've been surprised by the strength of my reactions to some of these objects as we've waded through our past. I've discovered and remembered things I had completely forgotten about.

By the time you read this it will have been many months since I last sat at the kitchen table in the house where I spent my life with my family. The walls of that home held me when I cried, echoed with our laughter and didn't tell on me when I snuck in or out as a teenager.

Our home kept all of our family memories contained in a safe, unshifting place. It's that place that I think of when I'm yearning for the comfort and warmth of home. Not my current family home where I'm raising my own unruly bunch—but where I was nurtured and admonished and felt the safest in the world. The place I always retreated to when I needed to feel connected to my roots, to my mum.

Conclusion

There was a lot that resurfaced during the packing and sorting of an entire lifetime of bits and pieces. It was like discovering a treasure trove of amazing things that elicited the greatest joy and sorrow at the same time. I wasn't expecting that. I never imagined that our family wouldn't be gathering in that kitchen in years to come, or that my children would no longer be running up and down the corridors and in and out of the garden. The connection to my mum and our precious family years was so deeply etched into the bricks of that home, and I took it for granted that it would be available to me forever.

It was unexpected, very sad and something I had absolutely no control over.

My last day at our family home was an incredibly emotional experience. I walked through each room in the house with my youngest child, who was newly walking and thrilled to be exploring the house on foot. Everything had been moved to the new house or to storage and the rooms stood empty. To me, though, the house still felt full. Each room was pulsing with memories, and I was flooded with a deep sadness and disbelief that this sanctuary and sacred, safe space would belong to somebody else by the morning.

I sat on the floor in the loungeroom, soaking in the last moments in the house as my littlest man toddled around me happily. It felt like the longest goodbye. In a way, it felt like I was saying goodbye to my mum for the final time. Once again, it was a goodbye that was out of my control, forced upon me without much warning.

As I closed the front door behind me for the last time I felt an immense sadness wash over me anew. But it was a different grief than that first one I went through, more than twenty years before. It was a settled, more mature sadness that didn't swell up in me kicking and screaming to be let out. It was familiar and comfortable, and I decided to let myself feel it. To give myself permission to be sad. To say that final goodbye to Mum; to farewell that chapter of our lives together.

As with all of the other plot twists in my life, the big and the small, I just had to roll with it—to swim in the ocean of feelings and try not to let myself drown. Which, with years of practice, I'm getting pretty good at now.

I hope that, with time, you will feel the same way about your own loss. I hope that when the next plot twist inevitably comes your way you will feel more confident in your ability to feel it and face it, secure in the knowledge that you will be okay.

It's also important to remember that not everything you read will apply to you. Take each idea as a concept to store away, to use as inspiration and to practise in your own life when it fits. Maybe you have a completely different way of processing the twists and turns of life. If it works for you, that is wonderful.

In reflecting on and sharing our experiences we are giving ourselves and the people around us the opportunity to blossom and grow, and to evolve with empathy and understanding. This is what connects us to our world, and helps us feel seen and heard.

I hope this book has reassured you that there is an arc through this process of loss and unexpected change—a beginning, a middle and a later stage where we've integrated our experiences. The force of the feelings and the impact of the shock can be blinding in the immediate aftermath, but with time, we can and we will find our way into a new kind of normal.

In all of the grief that surrounds these unexpected trials of life, it is also okay (and important) to grieve the person you once were. Like a snake shedding its skin and starting anew, or a butterfly emerging from the chrysalis, we can transform into a new version of ourselves without forgetting where we came from.

You don't have to go through any of this on your own. No matter how it may feel, you are not alone. There will always be people to catch you when you feel like you're falling—you just have to know who to ask. Talk to the people in your life, connect with like-minded communities or reach out to a therapist for some unbiased, non-judgemental, sacred space holding. Write and journal and find new ways to release your emotions. Share your thoughts and experiences with others.

Wishing you love, strength and courage as you take your next steps forward.

Acknowledgements

This book was written with the greatest, unwavering, most generous and enormous support from my publisher, Tessa Feggans. When I lost sight of the finish line (and most certainly lost faith in myself), or the direction or intention for the book, you guided me through it with confidence and an assurance that always left me thrumming with excitement and anticipation again. You truly are exceptional, and it has been such a privilege to work with you throughout this process. Thank you for every considered thought, email, meeting and phone call, and for all of your time and encouragement. I genuinely could not have done this without you.

I also could not have done this without the support of my manager, Dean Buchanan. Thank you for making this invaluable connection with Tessa and Allen & Unwin, for your patience and support and for being a sounding board when I'm in my own head.

A huge thank you also, to my copyeditor Brooke Lyons—what a gift you have been! Your comments and encouragement have been very much appreciated. It was a pleasure to read your notes and I really hope we get to work together again one day.

Thank you also to the lovely Greer Gamble for coordinating the entire editing process: you too have been a joy to work with and I am so grateful for your support.

To my beautiful partner Chris, for allowing me the time and the space to write when the house was literally falling down around us, and our three boys needed so much of our attention. As always, you have just taken it in your stride, picked up all the pieces, and without complaint (well, almost none) have lovingly wrangled, cleaned, cooked, arranged and provided our little circus with everything that we have needed to get through this busy time. I can't promise that I'll ever be as generous as you, but I can most certainly try! I love you and am so lucky to be walking through this life with you. Thank you for always encouraging me to follow my latest unbridled ventures.

Thank you to my family, for allowing me to share some of our stories here. This is a lot and I know it; thank you for trusting me with the retelling. In reliving and reflecting on so much of that early time, I am so proud of us. And I know she would be too.

Acknowledgements

To all of the beautiful people whose stories I have shared within the pages of this book—I am eternally grateful to have shared the space with you, whether in session, on a podcast or in conversation. Thank you for allowing me to use part of our time together to illuminate some of the ways that we can fall and get back up again in this complex and beautiful life.

A special thank you to 'Wendy in Advertising'—you know who you are—for always being a cheerleader and believer in all of the things that I do . . . or talk about doing. Our shared love of reality TV is my safe haven and escape, and the antidote to my stress. Thank you for always being there to receive my rants, to rant just as loudly and for our walk/chai/chip routine. A crucial part of the creative process, of course.

Another big thank you to my long-suffering colleague Dianne Anderson, who once again held down the fort, took on the clients, handled the revolving door of replacements and still managed to encourage me to follow my pursuits. I'm so grateful—you're the dream teammate.

And to my mum. All of this is because of you—almost everything I have become is because of the love and support that you gave me on earth, and everywhere I stumbled in the *after*. No matter how much further away we get from the time that we had together, those years in the *before* will always be the brightest. Thank you for allowing me to share some of my experiences with the world. Although I know that you would cover your face and shy away from the attention, I am grateful that despite all the hardships of grief and loss, there has been a glimmer of goodness that has grown out of it. I hope you're proud.

Resources

As a final note, although therapy is what I do as a profession and is often what I suggest or recommend, it's also important to remember that when the impact of a sudden plot twist lands us squarely in the discomfort zone, it is completely expected that we will feel anxious, distressed, in pain or despairing (and anything in between).

All of these feelings are entirely valid and a 'normal' response to our situation. Not all of these feelings or experiences require therapy to work through; sometimes, as you will have read, we just have to push through the pain, or wallow in the distress and move through it in our own time.

For some, though, these feelings may be more acute, and it can be important or even urgent to talk with a professional about them.

Please do not hesitate to reach out for help if you think you might need support.

Below is a list of resources that you may find useful.

Lifeline: 24/7 phone and online counselling support

Call any time on 13 11 14 or text chat via 0477 13 11 14

A 24/7 webchat option is also available via the website.

www.lifeline.org.au

Suicide Callback Service: 24/7 phone and online counselling support

1300 659 467

www.suicidecallbackservice.org.au

1800RESPECT: national domestic family and sexual violence counselling service

1800 737 732

www.1800respect.org.au

Beyond Blue: 24/7 mental health support for anxiety, depression and suicide

1300 22 4636 or webchat via the website.

www.beyondblue.org.au

13YARN: Aboriginal and Torres Strait Islander crisis support

13 92 76

www.13yarn.org.au

Blue Knot Foundation: complex trauma support

1300 657 380

www.blueknot.org.au

Relationships Australia: supporting respectful relationships

1300 364 277

www.relationships.org.au

Mensline: counselling support for men

1300 789 978

www.mensline.org.au

Parentline: counselling and support for parents and carers

13 22 89

https://services.dffh.vic.gov.au/parentline

Butterfly Foundation: eating disorders and body image support

1800 334 673 or chat online via the website.

www.butterfly.org.au

Or you can find an accredited psychotherapist, counsellor, family therapist, social worker or psychologist via:

www.goodtherapy.com.au/find_a_therapist.php